Easy Wedding Workbook & Organizer

The Most Useful
Wedding Planning Tool
Available Today!

By
Elizabeth & Alex Lluch
Professional Wedding Consultants

Written by

Elizabeth & Alex Lluch
Professional Wedding Consultants

Published by Wedding Solutions Publishing, Inc.
© Copyright 2000

Front Cover Photograph Provided By:
John Corbett, *John Corbett Photography*
928 West Main Road
Middletown, RI 02842
(401) 846-4861
www.corbettphotography.com

Back Cover Photographs Provided By:

<u>top left & bottom right:</u>	<u>bottom left & top right:</u>
Jon Barber	Karen French
Barber Photography	*Karen French Photography*
34085 Pacific Coast Highway #117	8351 Elmcrest
Dana Point, CA 92629	Huntington Beach, CA 92646
(949) 493-5840	(800) 734-6219
www.barberphotography.com	www.karenfrenchphotography.com
<u>middle left:</u>	<u>middle right:</u>
Carolyn Marie	Larry Monet
Carolyn Marie Photography	*Photography by Monet,*
9849 Dauntless Street	3708 Sixth Avenue
San Diego, CA 92126	San Diego, CA 92103
(619) 695-6852	(888) 827-7725
	www.photographybymonet.com

Cover Design By:
Amy Allen Graphics, San Diego, CA

Printed in China

ISBN 1-887169-14-8

 THE WEDDING OF

_____

_____

HO WILL BE MARRIED ON

_____

AT

_____

DEDICATED TO:

All brides and grooms.
May their wedding day be the
happiest day of their life!

CONTENTS

*I*NTRODUCTION

*D*ear Bride and Groom:

Congratulations on your engagement! You must be very excited for having found that special person to share the rest of your life with. And you must be looking forward to what will be the happiest day of your life -- your wedding! Planning your wedding can be fun and exciting. But it can also be very stressful. That is why Wedding Solutions Publishing, Inc., a professional wedding planning company, created *Easy Wedding Workbook & Organizer*.

Easy Wedding Workbook & Organizer contains over 140 worksheets to keep you organized and on top of your plans. *Easy Wedding Workbook & Organizer* also includes very detailed wedding planning checklists and a detailed budget analysis containing everything you need to do or consider when planning your wedding and the best time frame in which to accomplish each activity.

Following the wedding checklists and budget analysis are wedding timelines for your bridal party as well as your service providers. Use these timelines to keep everyone on schedule. You may also find our wedding party responsibility lists helpful in your planning. This list includes responsibilities for each member of your wedding party, a breakdown of who pays for what as well as the traditional formations for the ceremony, processional, recessional and receiving line for both Jewish and Christian weddings as well as the traditional seating arrangements at the reception.

The attached accordion file will allow you to organize your receipts, contracts, catalogs, brochures, samples, and other items that brides and grooms collect during their planning process.

We are confident that you will enjoy planning your wedding with the help of *Easy Wedding Workbook & Organizer*. So come join the many couples who have used this planner to plan a stress-free wedding. Also, if you have any suggestions or ideas that you would like to see included in this book, please write to us at: Wedding Solutions Publishing, Inc.; 6347 Caminito Tenedor; San Diego, CA 92120. We will include your ideas and suggestions in our next printing. We listen to brides and grooms like you!

Sincerely,

Elizabeth H. Lluch

*S*WEET *M*EMORIES

*T*HE *P*ROPOSAL

Date: _____   Time: _____

Location: _____   Proposed by: _____

He/She Said/Did: _____

_____

_____

_____

_____

_____

You Said/Did: _____

_____

_____

_____

_____

_____

Then We Did/Went To: _____

_____

_____

_____

_____

_____

BREAKING THE NEWS

My Parents' Reaction was: _____

_____

_____

_____

_____

_____

His/Her Parents' Reaction was: _____

_____

_____

_____

_____

_____

My Best Friend's Reaction was: _____

_____

_____

_____

_____

_____

His/Her Best Friend's Reaction was: _____

_____

_____

_____

_____

_____

Wedding Events at a Glance

Engagement Party Date: _____ Engagement Party Time: _____

Engagement Party Location: _____

Hostess: _____ Telephone Number: _____

Bridal Shower Date: _____ Bridal Shower Time: _____

Bridal Shower Location: _____

Hostess: _____ Telephone Number: _____

Bachelor Party Date: _____ Bachelor Party Time: _____

Bachelor Party Location: _____

Hostess: _____ Telephone Number: _____

Ceremony Rehearsal Date: _____ Ceremony Rehearsal Time: _____

Ceremony Rehearsal Location: _____

Contact Person: _____ Telephone Number: _____

Rehearsal Dinner Date: _____ Rehearsal Dinner Time: _____

Rehearsal Dinner Location: _____

Contact Person: _____ Telephone Number: _____

Ceremony Date: _____ Ceremony Time: _____

Ceremony Location: _____

Contact Person: _____ Telephone Number: _____

Reception Date: _____ Reception Time: _____

Reception Location: _____

Contact Person: _____ Telephone Number: _____

Information at a Glance

	Name	Contact Person	Telephone Number
Wedding Consultant			
Ceremony Site			
Officiant			
Reception Site			
Caterer			
Liquor Services			
Wedding Gown			
Tuxedo Rental			
Photographer			
Videographer			
Stationer			
Calligrapher			
Music (Ceremony)			
Music (Reception)			
Florist			
Bakery			
Decorations			
Ice Sculpture			
Party Favors			
Balloonist			
Transportation			
Rental & Supplies			
Gift Suppliers			
Valet Services			
Gift Attendant			
Rehearsal Dinner			

WEDDING PLANNING CHECKLIST

Nine Months and Earlier

- ❑ Announce your engagement.
- ❑ Select a date for your wedding.
- ❑ Hire a professional wedding consultant.
- ❑ Determine the type of wedding you want: location, formality, time of day, number of guests, etc.
- ❑ Determine budget and how expenses will be shared.
- ❑ Develop a record-keeping system for payments made.
- ❑ Consolidate all guest lists: bride's, groom's, bride's family, groom's family, and organize as follows:
    1) those who must be invited
    2) those who should be invited
    3) those who would be nice to invite
- ❑ Decide if you want to include children among guests.
- ❑ Select and reserve ceremony site.
- ❑ Select and reserve your officiant.
- ❑ Select and reserve reception site.
- ❑ Select and order your bridal gown and headpiece.
- ❑ Determine your color scheme.
- ❑ Send engagement notice with a photograph to your local newspaper.
- ❑ Buy a calendar and note all important activities: showers, luncheons, parties, get-togethers, etc.
- ❑ If ceremony or reception is at home, arrange for home or garden improvements as needed
- ❑ Select and book photographer.

- ❑ Order passport, visa or birth certificate, if needed for your honeymoon or marriage license.
- ❑ Select maid of honor, best man, bridesmaids and ushers
- ❑ (approx. one usher per 50 guests).

Six to Nine Months Before Wedding

- ❑ Select flower girl and ring bearer.
- ❑ Give the *Wedding Party Responsibility Cards* to your wedding party.
- ❑ Reserve wedding night bridal suite.
- ❑ Select attendants' dresses, shoes and accessories.
- ❑ Select flower girl's dress, shoes and accessories.
- ❑ Select and book caterer, if needed.
- ❑ Select and book ceremony musicians.
- ❑ Select and book reception musicians or DJ.
- ❑ Schedule fittings and delivery dates for yourself, attendants, flower girl and ring bearer.
- ❑ Select and book videographer.
- ❑ Select and book florist.

Four to Six Months Before Wedding

❑ Start shopping for each other's wedding gifts.

❑ Reserve rental items needed for ceremony & reception.

❑ Finalize guest list.

❑ Select and order wedding invitations, announcements and other stationery such as thank-you notes, wedding programs, and seating cards.

❑ Set date, time and location for your rehearsal dinner.

❑ Arrange accommodations for out-of- town guests.

❑ Start planning your honeymoon.

❑ Select and book all miscellaneous services, i.e. gift attendant, valet parking, etc. Register for gifts.

❑ Purchase shoes & accessories.

❑ Begin to break-in your shoes.

Two to Four Months Before Wedding

❑ Select bakery and order wedding cake.

❑ Order party favors.

❑ Select and order room decorations.

❑ Purchase honeymoon attire & luggage.

❑ Select and book transportation for wedding day.

❑ Check blood test and marriage license requirements.

❑ Shop for wedding rings and engrave them.

❑ Consider having your teeth cleaned or bleached.

❑ Consider writing a will and/or prenuptial agreement.

❑ Plan activities for your out-of-town guests both before and after the wedding.

❑ Purchase gifts for wedding attendants.

Six to Eight Weeks Before Wedding

❑ Mail invitations. Include accommodation choices and a map to assist guests in finding the ceremony and reception sites.

❑ Maintain a record of RSVPs and all gifts received. Send thank-you notes upon receipt of gifts.

❑ Determine hair style and makeup.

❑ Schedule to have your hair, makeup and nails done the day of the wedding.

❑ Finalize shopping for wedding day accessories such as toasting glasses, ring pillow, guest book, etc.

❑ Set up an area or a table in your home to display gifts as you receive them.

❑ Check with your local newspapers for wedding announcement requirements.

❑ Have your formal wedding portrait taken.

❑ Send wedding announcement & photograph to your local newspapers.

❑ Select and reserve wedding attire for groom, ushers, father of the bride and ring bearer.

Six to Eight Weeks Before Wedding
(Cont.)

❑ Change name & address on drivers license, social security card, insurance policies, subscriptions, bank accounts, memberships, etc.

❑ Select a guest book attendant. Decide where and when to have guests sign in.

❑ Mail invitations to rehearsal dinner.

❑ Get blood test and health certificate.

❑ Obtain marriage license.

❑ Plan a luncheon or dinner with your bridesmaids. Give them their gifts at that time or at the rehearsal dinner.

❑ Find "something old, something new, something borrowed, something blue, and a six pence (or shiny penny) for your shoe."

❑ Finalize your menu, beverage and alcohol order.

Two to Six Weeks Before Wedding

❑ Confirm ceremony details with your officiant.

❑ Arrange final fitting of bridesmaids' dresses.

❑ Have final fitting of your gown and headpiece.

❑ Make final floral selections.

❑ Pick up rings and check for fit.

❑ Finalize rehearsal dinner plans; arrange seating and write names on place cards, if desired.

❑ Make a detailed timeline for your wedding party.

❑ Make a detailed timeline for your service providers.

❑ Confirm details with all service providers, including attire. Give them a copy of your wedding timeline.

❑ Start packing for your honeymoon.

❑ Finalize addressing and stamping announcements.

❑ Decide if you want to form a receiving line. If so, determine when and where to form the line.

❑ Contact guests who haven't responded.

❑ Meet with photographer and confirm special photos you want.

❑ Meet with videographer and confirm special events or people you want videotaped.

❑ Meet with musicians and confirm music to be played during special events such as first dance.

❑ Continue writing thank-you notes as gifts arrive.

❑ Remind bridesmaids and ushers of when and where to pick up their wedding attire.

❑ Purchase the lipstick, nail polish and any other accessories you want your bridesmaids to wear.

❑ Determine ceremony seating for special guests. Give a list to the ushers.

❑ Plan reception room layout and seating with your reception site manager or caterer. Write names on place cards for arranged seating.

The Last Week

❑ Pick up wedding attire and make sure everything fits.

❑ Do final guest count and notify your caterer or reception site manager.

❑ Gather everything you will need for the rehearsal and wedding day as listed in the *Wedding Party Responsibility Cards*.

❑ Arrange for someone to drive the getaway car.

❑ Review the schedule of events and last minute arrangements with your service providers.

❑ Confirm all honeymoon reservations and accommodations. Pick up tickets and travelers checks.

❑ Finish packing your suitcases for the honeymoon.

❑ Familiarize yourself with guests' names. It will help during the receiving line and reception.

❑ Have the Post Office hold your mail while you are away on your honeymoon.

The Rehearsal Day

❑ Review list of things to bring to the rehearsal as listed in the *Wedding Party Responsibility Cards*.

❑ Put suitcases in getaway car.

❑ Give your bridesmaids the lipstick, nail polish and accessories you want them to wear for the wedding.

❑ Give best man the officiant's fee and any other checks for service providers. Instruct him to deliver these checks the day of the wedding.

❑ Arrange for someone to bring accessories such as flower basket, ring pillow, guest book & pen, toasting glasses, cake cutting knife and napkins to the ceremony and reception.

❑ Arrange for someone to mail announcements the day after the wedding.

❑ Arrange for someone to return rental items such as tuxedos, slip and cake pillars after the wedding.

❑ Provide each member of your wedding party with a detailed schedule of events for the wedding day.

❑ Review ceremony seating with ushers.

The Wedding Day

❑ Review list of things to bring to the ceremony as listed in the *Wedding Party Responsibility Cards*.

❑ Give the groom's ring to the maid of honor. Give the bride's ring to the best man.

❑ Simply follow your detailed schedule of events.

❑ Relax and enjoy your wedding!

PERSONAL NOTES

BUDGET ANALYSIS

This comprehensive Budget Analysis has been designed to provide you with all the expenses that can be incurred in any size wedding, including such hidden costs as taxes, gratuities and other "items" that can easily add up to thousands of dollars in a wedding. After you have completed this budget, you will have a much better idea of what your wedding will cost. You can then prioritize and allocate your expenses accordingly.

This budget is divided into fifteen categories: Ceremony, Wedding Attire, Photography, Videography, Stationery, Reception, Music, Bakery, Flowers, Decorations, Transportation, Rental Items, Gifts, Parties, and Miscellaneous. Categories or items written in italics are typically paid for by the groom or his family.

At the beginning of each category is the percentage of the total wedding budget that is typically spent in that category, based on national averages. Multiply your intended wedding budget by this percentage and write that amount in the "typical" space provided.

To determine the total cost of your wedding, estimate the amount of money you will spend on each item in the budget analysis and write that amount in the "Budget" column after each item. Next to each expense item is the page number where you can find detailed information about that item. Items printed in italics are traditionally paid for by the groom or his family.

Add all the "Budget" amounts within each category and write the total amount in the "Budget Subtotal" space at the end of each category. Then add all the "Subtotal" figures to come up with your final wedding budget. The "Actual" column is for you to input your actual expenses as you purchase items or hire your service providers. Writing down the actual expenses will help you stay within your budget.

For example, if your total wedding budget is $10,000, write this amount at the top of page 22. To figure your typical ceremony expenses, multiply $10,000 x .05 (5%) = $500.00. Write this amount on the "Typical" line in the "Ceremony" category to serve as a guide for all your ceremony expenses.

If you find, after adding up all your "Budget Subtotals," that the total amount is more than what you had in mind to spend, simply decide which items are more important to you and adjust your expenses accordingly.

CHECKLIST OF BUDGET ITEMS

CEREMONY

- ☐ Ceremony Site Fee
- ☐ *Officiant's Fee*
- ☐ *Officiant's Gratuity*
- ☐ Guest Book, Pen
- ☐ Penholder
- ☐ Ring Bearer Pillow
- ☐ Flower Girl Basket

WEDDING ATTIRE

- ☐ Bridal Gown
- ☐ Alterations
- ☐ Headpiece & Veil
- ☐ Gloves
- ☐ Jewelry
- ☐ Stockings
- ☐ Garter
- ☐ Shoes
- ☐ Hairdresser
- ☐ Makeup Artist
- ☐ Manicure/Pedicure
- ☐ *Groom's Formal Wear*

PHOTOGRAPHY

- ☐ Bride & Groom's Album
- ☐ Parents' Album
- ☐ Extra Prints
- ☐ Proofs/Previews

PHOTOGRAPHY (Cont.)

- ☐ Negatives
- ☐ Engagement Photograph
- ☐ Formal Bridal Portrait

VIDEOGRAPHY

- ☐ Main Video
- ☐ Titles
- ☐ Extra Hours
- ☐ Photo Montage
- ☐ Extra Copies

STATIONERY

- ☐ Invitations
- ☐ Response Cards
- ☐ Reception Cards
- ☐ Ceremony Cards
- ☐ Pew Cards
- ☐ Seating/Place Cards
- ☐ Rain Cards/Maps
- ☐ Ceremony Programs
- ☐ Announcements
- ☐ Thank-You Notes
- ☐ Stamps
- ☐ Calligraphy
- ☐ Napkins/ Matchbooks

RECEPTION

- ☐ Reception Site Fee
- ☐ Hors D' Oeuvres
- ☐ Main Meal/Caterer
- ☐ Liquor/ Beverages
- ☐ Bartending Fee
- ☐ Bar Set-up Fee
- ☐ Corkage Fee
- ☐ Fee to Pour Coffee
- ☐ Service Providers' Meals
- ☐ Gratuity
- ☐ Party Favors
- ☐ Disposable Cameras
- ☐ Rose Petals/Rice
- ☐ Gift Attendant
- ☐ Parking Fee
- ☐ Valet Services

MUSIC

- ☐ Ceremony Music
- ☐ Reception Music

BAKERY

- ☐ Wedding Cake
- ☐ *Groom's Cake*
- ☐ Cake Delivery
- ☐ Set-up Fee
- ☐ Cake-Cutting Fee
- ☐ Cake Top
- ☐ Cake Knife/Toast Glasses

*   Items in italics are traditionally paid for by the groom or his family

CHECKLIST OF BUDGET ITEMS (CONT.)

FLOWERS

Bouquets

☐ *Bride's*
☐ Tossing
☐ Maid of Honor's
☐ Bridesmaids'

Floral Hairpiece

☐ Maid of Honor
☐ Bridesmaids'
☐ Flower Girl's

Corsages

☐ *Bride's Going Away*
☐ *Other Family Members'*

Boutonnieres

☐ *Groom's*
☐ *Ushers*
☐ *Other Family's*

Ceremony Site
☐ Main Altar
☐ Alter Candelabra
☐ Aisle Pews

FLOWERS (Cont.)

Reception Site

☐ Reception Site
☐ Head Table
☐ Guest Tables
☐ Buffet Table
☐ Punch Table
☐ Cake Table
☐ Cake
☐ Cake Knife
☐ Toasting Glasses
☐ Floral Delivery & Setup

DECORATIONS

☐ Table Centerpieces
☐ Balloons

TRANSPORTATION

☐ Transportation

RENTAL ITEMS

☐ Bridal Slip
☐ Ceremony Accessories
☐ Tent/Canopy

RENTAL ITEMS (Cont.)

☐ Dance Floor
☐ Tables/Chairs
☐ Linen/Tableware
☐ Heaters
☐ Lanterns

GIFTS

☐ *Bride's Gift*
☐ Groom's Gift
☐ Bridesmaids' Gifts
☐ *Ushers' Gifts*

PARTIES

☐ Bridesmaids' Luncheon
☐ *Rehearsal Dinner*

MISCELLANEOUS

☐ Newspaper Announ.
☐ *Marriage License*
☐ *Prenuptial Agreement*
☐ Bridal Gown/Bouquet
☐ Preservation
☐ Wedding Consultant
☐ Wedding Software
☐ Taxes

* Items in italics are traditionally paid for by the groom or his family

BUDGET ANALYSIS

	BUDGET	ACTUAL
Your Total Wedding Budget	$	$
CEREMONY (Typical = 5% of Budget)		
Ceremony Site Fee	$	$
Officiant's Fee	$	$
Officiant's Gratuity	$	$
Guest Book, Pen, Penholder	$	$
Ring Bearer Pillow	$	$
Flower Girl Basket	$	$
Subtotal 1	$	$
WEDDING ATTIRE (Typical = 10% of Budget)		
Bridal Gown	$	$
Alterations	$	$
Headpiece & Veil	$	$
Gloves	$	$
Jewelry	$	$
Stockings	$	$
Garter	$	$
Shoes	$	$
Hairdresser	$	$
Makeup Artist	$	$
Manicure/Pedicure	$	$
Groom's Formal Wear	$	$
Subtotal 2	$	$

* Items in italics are traditionally paid for by the groom or his family

	BUDGET	ACTUAL
PHOTOGRAPHY (Typical = 9% of Budget)		
Bride & Groom's Album	$	$
Parents' Album	$	$
Extra Prints	$	$
Proofs/Previews	$	$
Negatives	$	$
Engagement Photograph	$	$
Formal Bridal Portrait	$	$
Subtotal 3	$	$
VIDEOGRAPHY (Typical = 5% of Budget)	$	$
Main Video	$	$
Titles	$	$
Extra Hours	$	$
Photo Montage	$	$
Extra Copies	$	$
Subtotal 4	$	$
STATIONERY (Typical = 4% of Budget)		
Invitations	$	$
Response Cards	$	$
Reception Cards	$	$
Ceremony Cards	$	$
Pew Cards	$	$
Seating/Place Cards	$	$
Rain Cards/Maps	$	$
Ceremony Programs	$	$
Announcements	$	$
Thank-You Notes	$	$

* Items in italics are traditionally paid for by the groom or his family

	BUDGET	ACTUAL
STATIONERY (CONT.)		
Stamps	$	$
Calligraphy	$	$
Napkins and Matchbooks	$	$
Subtotal 5	$	$
RECEPTION (Typical = 35% of Budget)		
Reception Site Fee	$	$
Hors D' Oeuvres	$	$
Main Meal/Caterer	$	$
Liquor/ Beverages	$	$
Bartending/Bar Set-up Fee	$	$
Corkage Fee	$	$
Fee To Pour Coffee	$	$
Service Providers' Meals	$	$
Gratuity	$	$
Party Favors/Disposable Cameras	$	$
Rose Petals/Rice	$	$
Gift Attendant	$	$
Parking Fee/Valet Services	$	$
Subtotal 6	$	$
MUSIC (Typical = 5% of Budget)		
Ceremony Music	$	$
Reception Music	$	$
Subtotal 7	$	$

*   Items in italics are traditionally paid for by the groom or his family

	BUDGET	ACTUAL
BAKERY (Typical = 2% of Budget)	$	$
Wedding Cake	$	$
Groom's Cake	$	$
Cake Delivery & Set-up Fee	$	$
Cake-Cutting Fee	$	$
Cake Top, Cake Knife, Toasting Glasses	$	$
Subtotal 8	$	$
FLOWERS (Typical = 6% of Budget)		
BOUQUETS		
Bride's	$	$
Tossing	$	$
Maid of Honor's	$	$
Bridesmaids'	$	$
FLORAL HAIRPIECES		
Maid of Honor/ Bridesmaids'	$	$
Flower Girl's	$	$
CORSAGES		
Bride's Going Away	$	$
Other Family Members'	$	$
BOUTONNIERES		
Groom's	$	$
Ushers and Other Family's	$	$
CEREMONY SITE FLOWERS		
Main Altar	$	$
Alter Candelabra	$	$
Aisle Pews	$	$

*   Items in italics are traditionally paid for by the groom or his family

	BUDGET	ACTUAL
RECEPTION SITE FLOWERS	$	$
Reception Site	$	$
Head Table	$	$
Guest Tables	$	$
Buffet Table	$	$
Punch Table	$	$
Cake Table	$	$
Cake	$	$
Cake Knife	$	$
Toasting Glasses	$	$
Floral Delivery & Setup	$	$
Subtotal 9	$	$
DECORATIONS (Typical = 3% of Budget)		
Table Centerpieces	$	$
Balloons	$	$
Subtotal 10	$	$
TRANSPORTATION (Typical = 2% of Budget)		
Transportation	$	$
Subtotal 11	$	$
RENTAL ITEMS (Typical = 3% of Budget)		
Bridal Slip	$	$
Ceremony Accessories	$	$
Tent/Canopy	$	$
Dance Floor	$	$
Tables/Chairs	$	$

*   Items in italics are traditionally paid for by the groom or his family

	BUDGET	ACTUAL
RENTAL ITEMS (CONT.)		
Linen/Tableware	$	$
Heaters, Lanterns, Other	$	$
Subtotal 12	$	$
GIFTS (Typical = 3% of Budget)		
Bride's/Groom's *Gift*	$	$
Bridesmaids'/ *Ushers' Gifts*	$	$
Subtotal 13		
PARTIES (Typical = 4% of Budget)		
Bridesmaids' Luncheon	$	$
Rehearsal Dinner	$	$
Subtotal 14		
MISCELLANEOUS (Typical = 4% of Budget)		
Newspaper Announcements	$	$
Marriage License	$	$
Prenuptial Agreement	$	$
Bridal Gown/Bouquet Preservation	$	$
Wedding Consultant	$	$
Wedding Planning Software	$	$
Taxes	$	$
Subtotal 15		
GRAND TOTAL (Add "Budget" & "Actual" Subtotals 1-15)	$	$

* Items in italics are traditionally paid for by the groom or his family

Vendor Payment Tracking Chart

	Business Name & Phone No.	Contract Date & Total Cost	Deposit & Date	Next Pay. & Date	Final Pay. & Date
Wedding Consultant					
Ceremony Site					
Officiant					
Reception Site					
Caterer					
Liquor Services					
Wedding Gown					
Tuxedo Rental					
Photographer					
Videographer					
Stationer					
Calligrapher					
Music (Ceremony)					
Music (Reception)					
Florist					
Bakery					
Decorations					
Ice Sculpture					
Party Favors					
Balloonist					
Transportation					
Rental & Supplies					
Gift Suppliers					
Valet Services					
Gift Attendant					
Rehearsal Dinner					

CEREMONY

Ceremony Site Comparison Chart

QUESTIONS	POSSIBILITY 1	POSSIBILITY 2
What is the name of the ceremony site?		
What is the address of the ceremony site?		
What is the name & phone number of my contact person?		
What dates & times are available?		
Do vows need to be approved?		
What is the ceremony site fee?		
What is the payment policy?		
What is the cancellation policy?		
Does the facility have liability insurance?		
What are the minimum & maximum number of guests allowed?		
What is the denomination, if any, of the facility?		
What restrictions are there with regards to denomination?		
Is an officiant available? At what cost?		
Are outside officiants allowed?		
Are any musical instruments available for our use?		
If so, what is the fee?		

CEREMONY 31

CEREMONY SITE COMPARISON CHART

POSSIBILITY 3	POSSIBILITY 4	POSSIBILITY 5

Ceremony Site Comparison Chart (CONT.)

QUESTIONS	POSSIBILITY 1	POSSIBILITY 2
What music restrictions are there, if any?		
What photography restrictions are there, if any?		
What videography restrictions are there, if any?		
Are there are any restrictions for rice or rose petal-tossing?		
Are candlelight ceremonies allowed?		
What floral decorations are available/allowed?		
When is my rehearsal to be scheduled?		
Is there handicap accessibility and parking?		
How many parking spaces are available for my wedding party?		
Where are they located?		
How many parking spaces are available for my guests?		
What rental items are necessary?		

CEREMONY SITE COMPARISON CHART (CONT.)

POSSIBILITY 3	POSSIBILITY 4	POSSIBILITY 5

Ceremony Reading Selections

SOURCE	SELECTION	READ BY	WHEN

Ceremony Music Selections

WHEN	SELECTION	AUTHOR	PLAYED BY
Prelude			
Prelude			
Processional			
Bride's Processional			
Ceremony			
Ceremony			
Recessional			
Postlude			

PERSONALIZED VOWS

Bride's Vows

_____
_____
_____
_____
_____
_____
_____
_____
_____

Groom's Vows

_____
_____
_____
_____
_____
_____
_____
_____
_____

PERSONALIZED RING CEREMONY

_____
_____
_____
_____
_____
_____
_____
_____

PEW SEATING ARRANGEMENTS

(Complete this form only after finalizing your guest list)

BRIDE'S FAMILY SECTION

PEW 1	PEW 2	PEW 3
_____	_____	_____
_____	_____	_____
_____	_____	_____
_____	_____	_____
_____	_____	_____
_____	_____	_____
_____	_____	_____
_____	_____	_____

PEW 4	PEW 5	PEW 6
_____	_____	_____
_____	_____	_____
_____	_____	_____
_____	_____	_____
_____	_____	_____
_____	_____	_____
_____	_____	_____
_____	_____	_____

PEW 7	PEW 8	PEW 9
_____	_____	_____
_____	_____	_____
_____	_____	_____
_____	_____	_____
_____	_____	_____
_____	_____	_____
_____	_____	_____

PEW SEATING ARRANGEMENTS

(Complete this form only after finalizing your guest list)

GROOM'S FAMILY SECTION

PEW 1   PEW 2   PEW 3

_____   _____   _____
_____   _____   _____
_____   _____   _____
_____   _____   _____
_____   _____   _____
_____   _____   _____
_____   _____   _____
_____   _____   _____

PEW 4   PEW 5   PEW 6

_____   _____   _____
_____   _____   _____
_____   _____   _____
_____   _____   _____
_____   _____   _____
_____   _____   _____
_____   _____   _____
_____   _____   _____

PEW 7   PEW 8   PEW 9

_____   _____   _____
_____   _____   _____
_____   _____   _____
_____   _____   _____
_____   _____   _____
_____   _____   _____
_____   _____   _____

Personal Notes

WEDDING ATTIRE

Wedding Attire

Bridal Gown

Options: Use the following guidelines to select customary attire for the groom:

Informal wedding:
Street-length gown or suit
Corsage or small bouquet
No veil or train

Semi-formal wedding:
Floor-length gown
Chapel train
Finger-tip veil
Small bouquet

Formal daytime wedding:
Floor-length gown
Chapel or sweep train
Fingertip veil or hat
Gloves
Medium-sized bouquet

Formal evening wedding: Same as formal daytime except longer veil

Very formal wedding:
Floor-length gown
Cathedral train
Full-length veil
Elaborate headpiece
Long sleeves or long arm-covering gloves
Cascading bouquet

GROOM'S FORMAL WEAR

Options: Use the following guidelines to select customary attire for the groom:

Informal wedding: Business suit
                                 White dress shirt and tie

Semi-formal daytime: Formal suit
                                 White dress shirt
                                 Cummerbund or vest
                                 Four-in-hand or bow tie

Semi-formal evening: Formal suit or dinner jacket
                                 Matching trousers
                                 White shirt
                                 Cummerbund or vest
                                 Black bow tie
                                 Cufflinks and studs

Formal daytime: Cutaway or stroller jacket
                                 Waistcoat
                                 Striped trousers
                                 White wing-collared shirt
                                 Striped tie
                                 Studs and cufflinks

Formal evening: Black dinner jacket
                                 Matching trousers
                                 Waistcoat
                                 White tuxedo shirt
                                 Bow tie
                                 Cummerbund or vest
                                 Cufflinks

Very formal daytime: Cutaway coat
Wing-collared shirt
Ascot
Striped trousers
Cufflinks
Gloves

Very formal evening: Black tailcoat
Matching striped trousers
Bow tie
White wing-collared shirt
Waistcoat
Patent leather shoes
Studs and cufflinks
Gloves

Bride's Attire Checklist

ITEM	DESCRIPTION	SOURCE
Full Slip	_____	_____
Garter	_____	_____
Gloves	_____	_____
Gown	_____	_____
Handbag	_____	_____
Jewelry	_____	_____
Lingerie	_____	_____
Pantyhose	_____	_____
Petticoat or Slip	_____	_____
Shoes	_____	_____
Something Old	_____	_____
Something New	_____	_____
Something Borrowed	_____	_____
Something Blue	_____	_____
Stocking	_____	_____
Veil/Hat	_____	_____

Bridal Boutique Comparison Chart

QUESTIONS	POSSIBILITY 1	POSSIBILITY 2
What is the name of the bridal boutique?		
What is the address of the bridal boutique?		
What is the name & phone number of my contact person?		
What are your hours of operation? Are appointments needed?		
Do you offer any discounts or give-aways?		
What major bridal gown lines do you carry?		
Do you carry outfits for the mother of the bride?		
Do you carry bridesmaids gowns and/or tuxedos?		
Do you carry outfits for the flower girl and ring bearer?		
What is the cost of the desired bridal gown?		
What is the cost of the desired headpiece?		
Do you offer in-house alterations? If so, what are your fees?		
Do you carry bridal shoes? What is their price range?		
Do you dye shoes to match outfits?		
Do you rent bridal slips? If so, what is the rental fee?		
What is the estimated date of delivery for my gown?		
What is your payment policy/cancellation policy?		

$\mathscr{B}$RIDAL $\mathscr{B}$OUTIQUE $\mathscr{C}$OMPARISON $\mathscr{C}$HART

POSSIBILITY 3	POSSIBILITY 4	POSSIBILITY 5

Bridal Attire Information Sheet

BRIDAL ATTIRE

Bridal Boutique _____ Date Ordered _____

Salesperson _____ Phone No. _____

Address _____

	Manufacturer	Style	Size	Cost	Date Ready	Pick-up Date
Wedding Gown						
Headpiece						
Veil/Hat						
Shoes						

GOWN ALTERATIONS

Location _____ Cost _____

Tailor _____ Phone No. _____

Address _____

	Date	Time
First Alteration		
Second Alteration		
Third Alteration		
Final Alteration		

Bridesmaids' Attire

BRIDESMAIDS' ATTIRE

Bridal Boutique _____   Date Ordered _____

Salesperson _____   Phone No. _____

Address _____   Cost _____

Description of dress _____

Manufacturer _____   Date ready _____

BRIDESMAIDS' SIZES

Name	Dress	Head	Weight	Height	Waist	Gloves	Shoes	Hose

Groomsmen's Attire

GROOMSMEN'S ATTIRE

Store Name _____ Date Ordered _____

Sales Person _____ Phone No. _____

Address _____ Cost _____

Description of tuxedo _____

Manufacturer _____ Date ready _____

GROOMSMEN'S SIZES

Name	Height	Weight	Waist	Sleeve	Inseam	Jacket	Neck	Shoes

PHOTOGRAPHY

Photographers Comparison Chart

QUESTIONS	POSSIBILITY 1	POSSIBILITY 2
What is the name & phone number of the photographer?		
What is the address of the photographer?		
How many years of experience do you have as a photographer?		
What percentage of your business is dedicated to weddings?		
Approximately how many weddings have you photographed?		
Are you the person who will photograph my wedding?		
Will you bring an assistant with you to my wedding?		
How do you typically dress for weddings?		
Do you have a professional studio?		
What type of equipment do you use?		
Do you bring backup equipment with you to weddings?		
Do you visit the ceremony and reception sites prior to the wedding?		
Do you have liability insurance?		
Are you skilled in diffused lighting & soft focus?		
Can you take studio portraits?		

PHOTOGRAPHERS COMPARISON CHART (CONT.)

POSSIBILITY 3	POSSIBILITY 4	POSSIBILITY 5

Photographers Comparison Chart (cont.)

QUESTIONS	POSSIBILITY 1	POSSIBILITY 2
Can you retouch negatives?		
Can negatives be purchased? If so, what is the cost?		
What is the cost of the package I am interested in?		
What is your payment policy?		
What is your cancellation policy?		
Do you offer a money-back guarantee?		
Do you use proofs?		
How many proofs will I get?		
When will I get my proofs?		
When will I get my album?		
What is the cost of an engagement portrait? Formal bridal portrait?		
What is the cost of a parent album?		
What is the cost of a 5" x 7" reprint?		
What is the cost of an 8" x 10" reprint?		
What is the cost of an 11" x 14" reprint?		
What is the cost per additional hour of shooting at the wedding?		

PHOTOGRAPHERS COMPARISON CHART (CONT.)

POSSIBILITY 3	POSSIBILITY 4	POSSIBILITY 5

Photographer's Information

(Make a copy of this form and give it to your photographer as a reminder of your various events).

THE WEDDING OF : _____   Tel. No.: _____

PHOTOGRAPHER'S COMPANY: _____

Address: _____

Photographer's Name: _____   Tel. No.: _____

Assistant's Name: _____   Tel. No.: _____

ENGAGEMENT PORTRAIT

Date: _____   Time: _____

Location: _____

Address: _____

BRIDAL PORTRAIT

Date: _____   Time: _____

Location: _____

Address: _____

PHOTOGRAPHER'S INFORMATION (Cont.)

(Make a copy of this form and give it to your photographer as a reminder of your various events).

OTHER EVENTS

Date: _____   Time: _____

Location: _____

Address: _____

CEREMONY

Date: _____   Arrival Time: _____   Departure Time: _____

Location: _____

Address: _____

Ceremony Restrictions/Guideline: _____

_____

RECEPTION

Date: _____   Arrival Time: _____   Departure Time: _____

Location: _____

Address: _____

Ceremony Restrictions/Guideline: _____

_____

$\mathcal{W}$EDDING $\mathcal{P}$HOTOS

(Make a copy of this form and give it to your photographer).

Pre-Ceremony Photos:

- ❏ Bride leaving her house
- ❏ Wedding rings with the invitation
- ❏ Bride getting dressed for the ceremony
- ❏ Bride looking at her bridal bouquet
- ❏ Maid of honor putting garter on bride's leg
- ❏ Groom and best man before ceremony
- ❏ Bride by herself
- ❏ Bride with her mother
- ❏ Bride with her father
- ❏ Bride with mother and father
- ❏ Bride with her entire family and/or any combination thereof
- ❏ Bride with her maid of honor
- ❏ Bride with her bridesmaids
- ❏ Bride with the flower girl and/or ring bearer
- ❏ Bride's mother putting on her corsage
- ❏ Groom leaving his house
- ❏ Groom putting on his boutonniere
- ❏ Groom with his mother
- ❏ Groom with his father
- ❏ Groom with mother and father
- ❏ Groom with his entire family and/or any combination thereof
- ❏ Groom with his best man
- ❏ Groom with his ushers
- ❏ Groom shaking hands with his best man while looking at his watch
- ❏ Groom with the bride's father
- ❏ Bride and her father getting out of the limousine
- ❏ Special members of the family being seated
- ❏ Groom waiting for the bride before the processional
- ❏ Bride and her father just before the processional

Other pre-ceremony photos you would like:

❑ _____
❑ _____
❑ _____
❑ _____
❑ _____

Ceremony Photos:

❑   The processional
❑   Bride and groom saying their vows
❑   Bride and groom exchanging rings
❑   Groom kissing the bride at the altar
❑   The recessional

Other ceremony photos you would like:

❑ _____
❑ _____
❑ _____
❑ _____
❑ _____

Post-Ceremony Photos:

❑   Bride and groom
❑   Newlyweds with both of their families
❑   Newlyweds with the entire wedding party
❑   Bride and groom signing the marriage certificate
❑   Flowers and other decorations

Other post-ceremony photos you would like:

❑ _____
❑ _____
❑ _____
❑ _____
❑ _____

Reception Photos:

- ❑ Entrance of newlyweds and wedding party into the reception site
- ❑ Receiving line
- ❑ Guests signing the guest book
- ❑ Toasts
- ❑ First dance
- ❑ Bride and her father dancing
- ❑ Groom and his mother dancing
- ❑ Bride dancing with groom's father
- ❑ Groom dancing with bride's mother
- ❑ Wedding party and guests dancing
- ❑ Cake table
- ❑ Cake-cutting ceremony
- ❑ Couple feeding each other cake
- ❑ Buffet table and its decoration
- ❑ Bouquet-tossing ceremony
- ❑ Garter-tossing ceremony
- ❑ Musicians
- ❑ The wedding party table
- ❑ The family tables
- ❑ Candid shots of your guests
- ❑ Bride and groom saying good-bye to their parents
- ❑ Bride and groom looking back, waiving good-bye in the getaway car

Other reception photos you would like:

- ❑ _____
- ❑ _____
- ❑ _____
- ❑ _____
- ❑ _____
- ❑ _____
- ❑ _____
- ❑ _____
- ❑ _____
- ❑ _____
- ❑ _____
- ❑ _____
- ❑ _____
- ❑ _____
- ❑ _____

VIDEOGRAPHY

Videographer Comparison Chart

QUESTIONS	POSSIBILITY 1	POSSIBILITY 2
What is the name & phone number of the videographer?		
What is the address of the videographer?		
How many years of experience do you have as a videographer?		
Approximately how many weddings have you videotaped?		
Are you the person who will videotape my wedding?		
Will you bring an assistant with you to my wedding?		
What type of equipment do you use?		
Do you have a wireless microphone?		
What format do you use (VHS, Super VHS, 8mm)?		
Do you bring backup equipment with you?		
Do you visit the ceremony and reception sites before the wedding?		
Do you edit the tape after the event? Who keeps the raw footage?		
When will I receive the final product?		
Cost of the desired package: What does it include?		
Can you make a photo montage? If so, what is your price?		
What is your payment policy? What is your cancellation policy?		
Do you offer a money-back guarantee?		

VIDEOGRAPHER COMPARISON CHART

POSSIBILITY 3	POSSIBILITY 4	POSSIBILITY 5

Personal Notes

_____

_____

_____

_____

_____

_____

_____

_____

_____

_____

_____

_____

_____

_____

_____

_____

_____

_____

_____

_____

_____

_____

_____

_____

_____

_____

_____

STATIONERY

Stationery

SAMPLES OF TRADITIONAL/FORMAL INVITATIONS

1)   When the bride's parents sponsor the wedding:

Mr. and Mrs. Alexander Waterman Smith
request the honor of your presence
at the marriage of their daughter
Carol Ann
to
Mr. William James Clark
on Saturday, the first of September
two thousand and one
at two o'clock in the afternoon
Saint James by-the-Sea
La Jolla, California

2)   When the groom's parents sponsor the wedding:

Mr. and Mrs. Michael Burdell Clark
request the honor of your presence
at the marriage of
Miss Carol Ann Smith
to their son
Mr. William James Clark

3)   When both the bride and groom's parents sponsor the wedding:

Mr. and Mrs. Alexander Waterman Smith
and
Mr. and Mrs. Michael Burdell Clark
request the honor of your presence
at the marriage of their children
Miss Carol Ann Smith
to
Mr. William James Clark

OR

Mr. and Mrs. Alexander Waterman Smith
request the honor of your presence
at the marriage of their daughter
Carol Ann Smith
to
William James Clark
son of Mr. and Mrs. Michael Burdell Clark

4)   When the bride and groom sponsor their own wedding:

The honor of your presence is requested
at the marriage of
Miss Carol Ann Smith
and
Mr. William James Clark

OR

Miss Carol Ann Smith
and
Mr. William James Clark
request the honor of your presence
at their marriage

5)   With divorced or deceased parents:

a) When the bride's mother is sponsoring the wedding and is not remarried:

Mrs. Julie Hurden Smith
requests the honor of your presence
at the marriage of her daughter
Carol Ann

b) When the bride's mother is sponsoring the wedding and has remarried:

Mrs. Julie Hurden Booker
requests the honor of your presence
at the marriage of her daughter
Carol Ann Smith

OR

Mr. and Mrs. John Thomas Booker
request the honor of your presence
at the marriage of Mrs. Booker's daughter
Carol Ann Smith

c) When the bride's father is sponsoring the wedding and has not remarried:

Mr. Alexander Waterman Smith
requests the honor of your presence
at the marriage of his daughter
Carol Ann

d) When the bride's father is sponsoring the wedding and has remarried:

Mr. and Mrs. Alexander Waterman Smith
request the honor of your presence
at the marriage of Mr. Smith's daughter
Carol Ann

6)   Deceased parents:

a) When a close friend or relative sponsors the wedding:

Mr. and Mrs. Brandt Elliott Lawson
request the honor of your presence
at the marriage of their granddaughter
Carol Ann Smith

7)   In military ceremonies, the rank determines the placement of names:

a) Any title lower than sergeant should be omitted. Only the branch of service should be included under that person's name:

Mr. and Mrs. Alexander Waterman Smith
request the honor of your presence
at the marriage of their daughter
Carol Ann
United States Army
to
William James Clark

b) Junior officers' titles are placed below their names and are followed by their branch of service:

> Mr. and Mrs. Alexander Waterman Smith
> request the honor of your presence
> at the marriage of their daughter
> Carol Ann
> to
> William James Clark
> First Lieutenant, United States Army

c) If the rank is higher than lieutenant, titles are placed before names, and the branch of service is placed on the following line:

> Mr. and Mrs. Alexander Waterman Smith
> request the honor of your presence
> at the marriage of their daughter
> Carol Ann
> to
> Captain William James Clark
> United States Navy

SAMPLE OF A LESS FORMAL MORE CONTEMPORARY INVITATION

> Mr. and Mrs. Alexander Waterman Smith
> would like you to
> join with their daughter
> Carol Ann
> and
> William James Clark
> in the celebration of their marriage

$\mathcal{R}$ESPONSE CARDS

Samples of wording for response cards:

M_____
(The M may be eliminated from the line, especially if many Drs. are invited)
___ accepts
___ regrets
Saturday the fifth of July
Oceanside Country Club

OR

The favor of your reply is requested
by the twenty-second of May
M_____
will _____ attend

$\mathcal{R}$ECEPTION CARDS

Sample of a formally-worded reception card:

Mr. and Mrs. Alexander Waterman Smith
request the pleasure of your company
Saturday, the third of July
at three o'clock
Oceanside Country Club
2020 Waterview Lane
Oceanside, California

Sample of a less formal reception card:

Reception immediately following the ceremony
Oceanside Country Club
2020 Waterview Lane
Oceanside, California

STATIONERY CHECKLIST

		QTY.	COST
❏	Invitations	_____	_____
❏	Envelopes	_____	_____
❏	Response Cards/Envelopes	_____	_____
❏	Reception Cards	_____	_____
❏	Ceremony Cards	_____	_____
❏	Pew Cards	_____	_____
❏	Seating/Place Cards	_____	_____
❏	Rain Cards	_____	_____
❏	Maps	_____	_____
❏	Ceremony Programs	_____	_____
❏	Announcements	_____	_____
❏	Thank-You Notes	_____	_____
❏	Stamps	_____	_____
❏	Personalized Napkins	_____	_____
❏	Personalized Matchbooks	_____	_____

Stationery Wording

Invitations

_____
_____
_____
_____
_____
_____
_____
_____
_____

Announcements

_____
_____
_____
_____
_____
_____

Reception Cards

_____
_____
_____
_____

Response Cards

_____
_____
_____

Seating/Pew Cards

_____
_____
_____

Napkins/Matchbooks

_____
_____
_____

Sample Ceremony Program

The Marriage of
Carol Ann Smith and William James Clark
the fourth of March, 2000
San Diego, California

OUR CEREMONY

Prelude:
All I Ask of You, by Andrew Lloyd Webber

Processional:
The Canon, by Pachelbel

Rite of Marriage

Welcome guests

Statement of intentions

Marriage vows

Exchange of rings

Blessing of bride and groom

Pronouncement of marriage

Presentation of the bride and groom

Recessional:
Trumpet Voluntary, by Jeromiah Clarke

SAMPLE CEREMONY PROGRAM (CONT.)

OUR WEDDING PARTY

Maid of Honor:
Susan Smith, Sister of Bride

Best Man:
Brandt Clark, Brother of Groom

Bridesmaids:
Janet Anderson, Friend of Bride
Lisa Bennett, Friend of Bride

Ushers:
Mark Gleason, Friend of Groom
Tommy Olson, Friend of Groom

Officiant:
Father Henry Thomas

OUR RECEPTION

Please join us after the ceremony
in the celebration of our marriage at:
La Valencia Hotel
1132 Prospect Street
La Jolla, CA

CEREMONY PROGRAM NOTES

STATIONERY COMPARISON CHART

QUESTIONS	POSSIBILITY 1	POSSIBILITY 2
What is the name & phone number of the stationery provider?		
What is the address of the stationery provider?		
How many years of experience do you have?		
What lines of stationery do you carry?		
What types of printing process do you offer?		
How soon in advance does the order have to be placed?		
What is the turn around time?		
What is the cost of the desired invitation? Announcement?		
What is the cost of the desired response card? Reception card?		
What is the cost of the desired thank-you note?		
What is the cost of the desired party favors?		
What is the cost of the desired wedding program?		
What is the cost of addressing the envelopes in calligraphy?		
What is your payment policy?		
What is your cancellation policy?		

STATIONERY COMPARISON CHART

POSSIBILITY 3	POSSIBILITY 4	POSSIBILITY 5

Stationery Description

Stationer _____   Date Ordered _____

Sales Person _____   Phone No. _____

Address _____

Invitations (Paper, Style, Color, Font, Printing)   _____

_____

Reception Cards (Paper, Style, Color, Font, Printing)   _____

_____

Response Cards (Paper, Style, Color, Font, Printing)   _____

_____

Announcements (Paper, Style, Color, Font, Printing)   _____

_____

Seating/Pew Cards (Paper, Style, Color, Font, Printing)   _____

_____

Napkins/Matchbooks (Paper, Style, Color, Font, Printing)   _____

_____

ADDRESSING ENVELOPES

GUIDELINES FOR ADDRESSING INVITATIONS

SITUATION	INNER ENVELOPE (no first name or address)	OUTER ENVELOPE (has first name and address)
Husband and Wife (with same surname)	Mr. and Mrs. Smith	Mr. and Mrs. Thomas Smith (use middle name, if known)
Husband and Wife (with different surnames)	Ms. Banks and Mr. Smith (wife first)	Ms. Anita Banks Mr. Thomas Smith (wife's name above husband's)
Husband and Wife (wife has professional title)	Dr. Smith and Mr. Smith	Dr. Anita Smith Mr. Thomas Smith (wife's name & title above husband's)
Husband and Wife (with Children under 16)	Mr. and Mrs. Smith John, Mary, and Glen (in order of age)	Mr. and Mrs. Thomas Smith
Single Woman (regardless of age)	Miss/Ms. Smith	Miss/Ms. Beverly Smith
Single Woman and Guest	Miss/Ms. Smith Mr. Jones (or "and Guest")	Miss/Ms. Beverly Smith
Single Man	Mr. Jones (Master for a young boy)	Mr. William Jones
Single Man and Guest	Mr. Jones Miss/Ms. Smith (or "and Guest")	Mr. William Jones
Unmarried Couple Living Together	Mr. Knight and Ms. Orlandi (names listed alphabetically)	Mr. Michael Knight Ms. Paula Orlandi
Two Sisters (over 16)	The Misses Smith	The Misses Mary and Jane Smith (in order of age)
Two Brothers (over 16)	The Messrs. Smith	The Messrs. John and Glen Smith (in order of age)
Brothers & Sisters (over 16)	Mary, Jane, John & Glen (name the girls first, in order of age)	The Misses Smith The Messrs. Smith (name the girls first)
A Brother and Sister (over 16)	Jane and John (name the girl first)	Miss Jane Smith and Mr. John Smith (name the girl first)
Widow	Mrs. Smith	Mrs. William Smith
Divorcee	Mrs. Smith	Mrs. Jones Smith (maiden name and former husband's surname)

Personal Notes

GUEST & GIFT LISTS

Guest & Gift List

Name Telephone No. Street Address City, State, Zip Code	Table # ——— Pew #	Rsvp How Many?	Shower Gift ——————— Wedding Gift	Thank You Sent
———————————— ———————————— ————————————	———		————————	
———————————— ———————————— ————————————	———		————————	
———————————— ———————————— ————————————	———		————————	
———————————— ———————————— ————————————	———		————————	
———————————— ———————————— ————————————	———		————————	
———————————— ———————————— ————————————	———		————————	
———————————— ———————————— ————————————	———		————————	
———————————— ———————————— ————————————	———		————————	

GUEST & GIFT LIST

Name Telephone No. Street Address City, State, Zip Code	Table # ——— Pew #	Rsvp How Many?	Shower Gift ———————— Wedding Gift	Thank You Sent
——————— ——————— ———————	——		———————	
——————— ——————— ———————	——		———————	
——————— ——————— ———————	——		———————	
——————— ——————— ———————	——		———————	
——————— ——————— ———————	——		———————	
——————— ——————— ———————	——		———————	
——————— ——————— ———————	——		———————	
——————— ——————— ———————	——		———————	

Guest & Gift List

Name Telephone No. Street Address City, State, Zip Code	Table # ——— Pew #	Rsvp How Many?	Shower Gift ———————— Wedding Gift	Thank You Sent
——————————— ——————————— ———————————	———		————————	
——————————— ——————————— ———————————	———		————————	
——————————— ——————————— ———————————	———		————————	
——————————— ——————————— ———————————	———		————————	
——————————— ——————————— ———————————	———		————————	
——————————— ——————————— ———————————	———		————————	
——————————— ——————————— ———————————	———		————————	
——————————— ——————————— ———————————	———		————————	

GUEST & GIFT LIST

Name Telephone No. Street Address City, State, Zip Code	Table # ——— Pew #	Rsvp How Many?	Shower Gift ——————— Wedding Gift	Thank You Sent
———————— ———————— ————————	———		————————	
———————— ———————— ————————	———		————————	
———————— ———————— ————————	———		————————	
———————— ———————— ————————	———		————————	
———————— ———————— ————————	———		————————	
———————— ———————— ————————	———		————————	
———————— ———————— ————————	———		————————	
———————— ———————— ————————	———		————————	

GUEST & GIFT LIST

Name Telephone No. Street Address City, State, Zip Code	Table # ——— Pew #	Rsvp How Many?	Shower Gift ——— Wedding Gift	Thank You Sent
——————— ——————— ———————	———		———————	
——————— ——————— ———————	———		———————	
——————— ——————— ———————	———		———————	
——————— ——————— ———————	———		———————	
——————— ——————— ———————	———		———————	
——————— ——————— ———————	———		———————	
——————— ——————— ———————	———		———————	
——————— ——————— ———————	———		———————	

GUEST & GIFT LIST

Name Telephone No. Street Address City, State, Zip Code	Table # ——— Pew #	Rsvp How Many?	Shower Gift ——— Wedding Gift	Thank You Sent
——————— ——————— ———————	———		———————	
——————— ——————— ———————	———		———————	
——————— ——————— ———————	———		———————	
——————— ——————— ———————	———		———————	
——————— ——————— ———————	———		———————	
——————— ——————— ———————	———		———————	
——————— ——————— ———————	———		———————	
——————— ——————— ———————	———		———————	

Guest & Gift List

Name Telephone No. Street Address City, State, Zip Code	Table # ——— Pew #	Rsvp How Many?	Shower Gift ——————— Wedding Gift	Thank You Sent
—————————— —————————— ——————————	———		——————————	
—————————— —————————— ——————————	———		——————————	
—————————— —————————— ——————————	———		——————————	
—————————— —————————— ——————————	———		——————————	
—————————— —————————— ——————————	———		——————————	
—————————— —————————— ——————————	———		——————————	
—————————— —————————— ——————————	———		——————————	
—————————— —————————— ——————————	———		——————————	

GUEST & GIFT LIST

Name Telephone No. Street Address City, State, Zip Code	Table # ——— Pew #	Rsvp How Many?	Shower Gift ——————— Wedding Gift	Thank You Sent
———————— ———————— ————————	———		———————	
———————— ———————— ————————			———————	
———————— ———————— ————————	———		———————	
———————— ———————— ————————	———		———————	
———————— ———————— ————————	———		———————	
———————— ———————— ————————	———		———————	
———————— ———————— ————————	———		———————	
———————— ———————— ————————	———		———————	

Guest & Gift List

Name Telephone No. Street Address City, State, Zip Code	Table # ——— Pew #	Rsvp How Many?	Shower Gift ——————— Wedding Gift	Thank You Sent
—————————— —————————— ——————————	———		———————	
—————————— —————————— ——————————	———		———————	
—————————— —————————— ——————————	———		———————	
—————————— —————————— ——————————	———		———————	
—————————— —————————— ——————————	———		———————	
—————————— —————————— ——————————	———		———————	
—————————— —————————— ——————————	———		———————	
—————————— —————————— ——————————	———		———————	

GUEST & GIFT LIST

Name Telephone No. Street Address City, State, Zip Code	Table # ——— Pew #	Rsvp How Many?	Shower Gift ——————— Wedding Gift	Thank You Sent
———————— ———————— ————————	———		————————	
———————— ———————— ————————	———		————————	
———————— ———————— ————————	———		————————	
———————— ———————— ————————	———		————————	
———————— ———————— ————————	———		————————	
———————— ———————— ————————	———		————————	
———————— ———————— ————————	———		————————	
———————— ———————— ————————	———		————————	

Guest & Gift List

Name Telephone No. Street Address City, State, Zip Code	Table # ——— Pew #	Rsvp How Many?	Shower Gift ——————— Wedding Gift	Thank You Sent
_____ _____ _____	___		_____	
_____ _____ _____	___		_____	
_____ _____ _____	___		_____	
_____ _____ _____	___		_____	
_____ _____ _____	___		_____	
_____ _____ _____	___		_____	
_____ _____ _____	___		_____	
_____ _____ _____	___		_____	

GUEST & GIFT LIST

Name Telephone No. Street Address City, State, Zip Code	Table # ——— Pew #	Rsvp How Many?	Shower Gift ——————— Wedding Gift	Thank You Sent
_____ _____ _____	___		_____	
_____ _____ _____	___		_____	
_____ _____ _____	___		_____	
_____ _____ _____	___		_____	
_____ _____ _____	___		_____	
_____ _____ _____	___		_____	
_____ _____ _____	___		_____	

ANNOUNCEMENT LIST

Name Telephone No. Street Address City, State, Zip Code	Name Telephone No. Street Address City, State, Zip Code

ANNOUNCEMENT LIST

Name Telephone No. Street Address City, State, Zip Code	Name Telephone No. Street Address City, State, Zip Code

Announcement List

Name Telephone No. Street Address City, State, Zip Code	Name Telephone No. Street Address City, State, Zip Code

ANNOUNCEMENT LIST

Name	Name
Telephone No.	Telephone No.
Street Address	Street Address
City, State, Zip Code	City, State, Zip Code

$\mathscr{G}$UEST $\mathscr{A}$CCOMMODATION $\mathscr{L}$IST

Name_____
Airline/Train_____
Pick Up By _____
Address _____
Cost Per Room _____
Departure Date _____ Time _____
Airline/Train _____

Arrival Date _____ Time _____
Flight/Train No. _____
Will Stay At _____
Phone No. _____
Confirmation No. _____
Taken By _____
Flight/Train No. _____

Name_____
Airline/Train_____
Pick Up By _____
Address _____
Cost Per Room _____
Departure Date _____ Time _____
Airline/Train _____

Arrival Date _____ Time _____
Flight/Train No. _____
Will Stay At _____
Phone No. _____
Confirmation No. _____
Taken By _____
Flight/Train No. _____

Name_____
Airline/Train_____
Pick Up By _____
Address _____
Cost Per Room _____
Departure Date _____ Time _____
Airline/Train _____

Arrival Date _____ Time _____
Flight/Train No. _____
Will Stay At _____
Phone No. _____
Confirmation No. _____
Taken By _____
Flight/Train No. _____

Name_____
Airline/Train_____
Pick Up By _____
Address _____
Cost Per Room _____
Departure Date _____ Time _____
Airline/Train _____

Arrival Date _____ Time _____
Flight/Train No. _____
Will Stay At _____
Phone No. _____
Confirmation No. _____
Taken By _____
Flight/Train No. _____

Name_____
Airline/Train_____
Pick Up By _____
Address _____
Cost Per Room _____
Departure Date _____ Time _____
Airline/Train _____

Arrival Date _____ Time _____
Flight/Train No. _____
Will Stay At _____
Phone No. _____
Confirmation No. _____
Taken By _____
Flight/Train No. _____

GUEST ACCOMMODATION LIST

Name_____   Arrival Date _____ Time _____
Airline/Train_____   Flight/Train No. _____
Pick Up By _____   Will Stay At _____
Address _____   Phone No. _____
Cost Per Room _____   Confirmation No. _____
Departure Date _____ Time _____   Taken By _____
Airline/Train _____   Flight/Train No. _____

Name_____   Arrival Date _____ Time _____
Airline/Train_____   Flight/Train No. _____
Pick Up By _____   Will Stay At _____
Address _____   Phone No. _____
Cost Per Room _____   Confirmation No. _____
Departure Date _____ Time _____   Taken By _____
Airline/Train _____   Flight/Train No. _____

Name_____   Arrival Date _____ Time _____
Airline/Train_____   Flight/Train No. _____
Pick Up By _____   Will Stay At _____
Address _____   Phone No. _____
Cost Per Room _____   Confirmation No. _____
Departure Date _____ Time _____   Taken By _____
Airline/Train _____   Flight/Train No. _____

Name_____   Arrival Date _____ Time _____
Airline/Train_____   Flight/Train No. _____
Pick Up By _____   Will Stay At _____
Address _____   Phone No. _____
Cost Per Room _____   Confirmation No. _____
Departure Date _____ Time _____   Taken By _____
Airline/Train _____   Flight/Train No. _____

Name_____   Arrival Date _____ Time _____
Airline/Train_____   Flight/Train No. _____
Pick Up By _____   Will Stay At _____
Address _____   Phone No. _____
Cost Per Room _____   Confirmation No. _____
Departure Date _____ Time _____   Taken By _____
Airline/Train _____   Flight/Train No. _____

Guest Accommodation List

Name_____   Arrival Date _____ Time _____
Airline/Train_____   Flight/Train No. _____
Pick Up By _____   Will Stay At _____
Address _____   Phone No. _____
Cost Per Room _____   Confirmation No. _____
Departure Date _____ Time _____ Taken By _____
Airline/Train _____   Flight/Train No. _____

Name_____   Arrival Date _____ Time _____
Airline/Train_____   Flight/Train No. _____
Pick Up By _____   Will Stay At _____
Address _____   Phone No. _____
Cost Per Room _____   Confirmation No. _____
Departure Date _____ Time _____ Taken By _____
Airline/Train _____   Flight/Train No. _____

Name_____   Arrival Date _____ Time _____
Airline/Train_____   Flight/Train No. _____
Pick Up By _____   Will Stay At _____
Address _____   Phone No. _____
Cost Per Room _____   Confirmation No. _____
Departure Date _____ Time _____ Taken By _____
Airline/Train _____   Flight/Train No. _____

Name_____   Arrival Date _____ Time _____
Airline/Train_____   Flight/Train No. _____
Pick Up By _____   Will Stay At _____
Address _____   Phone No. _____
Cost Per Room _____   Confirmation No. _____
Departure Date _____ Time _____ Taken By _____
Airline/Train _____   Flight/Train No. _____

Name_____   Arrival Date _____ Time _____
Airline/Train_____   Flight/Train No. _____
Pick Up By _____   Will Stay At _____
Address _____   Phone No. _____
Cost Per Room _____   Confirmation No. _____
Departure Date _____ Time _____ Taken By _____
Airline/Train _____   Flight/Train No. _____

GUEST ACCOMMODATION LIST

Name_____   Arrival Date _____ Time _____
Airline/Train_____   Flight/Train No. _____
Pick Up By _____   Will Stay At _____
Address _____   Phone No. _____
Cost Per Room _____   Confirmation No. _____
Departure Date _____ Time _____   Taken By _____
Airline/Train _____   Flight/Train No. _____

Name_____   Arrival Date _____ Time _____
Airline/Train_____   Flight/Train No. _____
Pick Up By _____   Will Stay At _____
Address _____   Phone No. _____
Cost Per Room _____   Confirmation No. _____
Departure Date _____ Time _____   Taken By _____
Airline/Train _____   Flight/Train No. _____

Name_____   Arrival Date _____ Time _____
Airline/Train_____   Flight/Train No. _____
Pick Up By _____   Will Stay At _____
Address _____   Phone No. _____
Cost Per Room _____   Confirmation No. _____
Departure Date _____ Time _____   Taken By _____
Airline/Train _____   Flight/Train No. _____

Name_____   Arrival Date _____ Time _____
Airline/Train_____   Flight/Train No. _____
Pick Up By _____   Will Stay At _____
Address _____   Phone No. _____
Cost Per Room _____   Confirmation No. _____
Departure Date _____ Time _____   Taken By _____
Airline/Train _____   Flight/Train No. _____

Name_____   Arrival Date _____ Time _____
Airline/Train_____   Flight/Train No. _____
Pick Up By _____   Will Stay At _____
Address _____   Phone No. _____
Cost Per Room _____   Confirmation No. _____
Departure Date _____ Time _____   Taken By _____
Airline/Train _____   Flight/Train No. _____

Receiving Line

To design your receiving line, simply place the names of the people you want included and the order in which you want them to stand.

When _____   Where _____

Traditional Receiving Line	**Your Receiving Line**
Mother of the Bride	_____
Father of the Bride (optional)	_____
Mother of the Groom	_____
Father of the Groom (optional)	_____
Bride	_____
Groom	_____
Maid of Honor	_____
Best Man	_____

Regardless of how you structure your receiving line, the mother of the bride is always first.

Close family members, bridesmaids, and ushers can also be included in the receiving line, if you wish.

Please note that for a large wedding (over 100 guests) we do not recommend a receiving line because it takes too long for your guests to go through it.

RECEPTION

Reception Site Comparison Chart

QUESTIONS	POSSIBILITY 1	POSSIBILITY 2
What is the name of the reception site?		
What is the address of the reception site?		
What is the name & phone number of my contact person?		
What dates & times are available?		
What is the maximum number of guests for a seated reception?		
What is the maximum number of guests for a cocktail reception?		
What is the reception site fee?		
What is the price range for a seated lunch?		
What is the price range for a buffet lunch?		
What is the price range for a seated dinner?		
What is the price range for a buffet dinner?		
What is the corkage fee?		
What is the cake-cutting fee?		
What is the ratio of servers to guests?		
How much time will be allotted for my reception?		
What music restrictions are there, if any?		
What alcohol restrictions are there, if any?		

RECEPTION SITE COMPARISON CHART

POSSIBILITY 3	POSSIBILITY 4	POSSIBILITY 5

Reception Site Comparison Chart (CONT.)

QUESTIONS	POSSIBILITY 1	POSSIBILITY 2
Are there any restrictions for rice or rose petal-tossing?		
What room and table decorations are available?		
Is a changing room available?		
Is there handicap accessibility?		
Is a dance floor included in the site fee?		
Are tables, chairs, and linens included in the site fee?		
Are outside caterers allowed?		
Are kitchen facilities available for outside caterers?		
Does the facility have full liability insurance?		
What "perks" or giveaways are offered?		
How many parking spaces are available for my wedding party?		
How many parking spaces are available for my guests?		
What is the cost for parking, if any?		
What is the cost for sleeping rooms, if available?		
What is the payment policy?		
What is the cancellation policy?		
Are credit cards accepted?		

RECEPTION SITE COMPARISON CHART (CONT.)

POSSIBILITY 3	POSSIBILITY 4	POSSIBILITY 5

Reception Information Sheet

RECEPTION SITE _____

Site Coordinator _____   Cost _____

Phone No. _____   Fax. No. _____

Address _____

Name of Room _____   Room Capacity _____

Date Confirmed _____   Confirm Head Count By _____

Beginning Time _____   Ending Time _____

Cocktails/Hors d'oeuvres Time _____   Meal Time _____

Color of Linens _____   Color of Napkins _____

TOTAL COST _____ Deposit _____ Date _____

Balance _____   Date Due_____

Cancellation Policy _____

EQUIPMENT INCLUDES:

   ❑ Tables   ❑ Chairs   ❑ Linens   ❑ Tableware
   ❑ Barware   ❑ Heaters   ❑ Electric Outlet   ❑ Musical Inst.

SERVICE INCLUDES:

   ❑ Waiters   ❑ Bartenders   ❑ Valet   ❑ Main Meal
   ❑ Cleanup   ❑ Setup   ❑ Security   ❑ Free Parking

CATERER INFORMATION SHEET

CATERER _____

Contact Person _____   Cost Per Person _____

Phone No. _____   Fax. No. _____

Address _____

Confirmed Date _____   Confirm Head Count By _____

Arrival Time _____   Departure Time _____

Cocktails/Hors d'oeuvres Time _____   Meal Time _____

Color of Linens _____   Color of Napkins _____

TOTAL COST _____   Deposit _____   Date _____

Balance _____   Date Due_____

Cancellation Policy _____

EQUIPMENT INCLUDES:

❏ Tables   ❏ Chairs   ❏ Linens   ❏ Tableware
❏ Barware   ❏ Heaters   ❏ Lighting   ❏ Candles

SERVICE INCLUDES:

❏ Waiters   ❏ Bartenders   ❏ Setup   ❏ Cleanup
❏ Security   ❏ Hors d'oeuvres ❏ Buffet Meal   ❏ Seated Meal
❏ Cocktails   ❏ Champagne   ❏ Wine   ❏ Beer
❏ Punch   ❏ Soft Drinks   ❏ Coffee/Tea   ❏ Cake

$\mathcal{T}$ABLE $\mathcal{S}$EATING $\mathcal{A}$RRANGEMENT

(Complete this form only after finalizing your guest list).

HEAD TABLE	BRIDE'S FAMILY TABLE	GROOM'S FAMILY TABLE
_____	_____	_____
_____	_____	_____
_____	_____	_____
_____	_____	_____
_____	_____	_____
_____	_____	_____
_____	_____	_____
_____	_____	_____

TABLE 1	TABLE 2	TABLE 3
_____	_____	_____
_____	_____	_____
_____	_____	_____
_____	_____	_____
_____	_____	_____
_____	_____	_____
_____	_____	_____
_____	_____	_____

TABLE 4	TABLE 5	TABLE 6
_____	_____	_____
_____	_____	_____
_____	_____	_____
_____	_____	_____
_____	_____	_____
_____	_____	_____
_____	_____	_____
_____	_____	_____

TABLE SEATING ARRANGEMENT

(Complete this form only after finalizing your guest list).

TABLE 7	TABLE 8	TABLE 9
_____	_____	_____
_____	_____	_____
_____	_____	_____
_____	_____	_____
_____	_____	_____
_____	_____	_____
_____	_____	_____
_____	_____	_____

TABLE 10	TABLE 11	TABLE 12
_____	_____	_____
_____	_____	_____
_____	_____	_____
_____	_____	_____
_____	_____	_____
_____	_____	_____
_____	_____	_____
_____	_____	_____

TABLE 13	TABLE 14	TABLE 15
_____	_____	_____
_____	_____	_____
_____	_____	_____
_____	_____	_____
_____	_____	_____
_____	_____	_____
_____	_____	_____
_____	_____	_____

Liquor Order Form

Liquor Store	_____	Date Ordered	_____
Salesperson	_____	Phone No.	_____
Address	_____	Cost	_____
Delivered by	_____	Delivery Date	_____

Type of Liquor	# of Bottles Needed	Price
_____	_____	_____
_____	_____	_____
_____	_____	_____
_____	_____	_____
_____	_____	_____
_____	_____	_____
_____	_____	_____
_____	_____	_____
_____	_____	_____
_____	_____	_____
_____	_____	_____

PARTY FAVORS COMPARISON CHART

	QUANTITY	PRICE
White matchboxes engraved with names of bride and groom and date of the wedding	_____	_____
Cocktail napkins engraved with names of the bride and groom and date of the wedding	_____	_____
Almonds, chocolates or other fine candy	_____	_____
Customized wine or champagne labels with bride and groom's names and wedding date	_____	_____
Porcelain or ceramic favors with bride and groom's names and wedding date	_____	_____
Plant or tree shoot to be planted in honor of the bride and groom	_____	_____

Caterer Comparison Chart

QUESTIONS	POSSIBILITY 1	POSSIBILITY 2
What is the name of the caterer?		
What is the address of the caterer?		
What is the name & phone number of my contact person?		
How many years have you been in business?		
What percentage of your business is dedicated to wedding receptions?		
Do you have liability insurance? Are you licensed to serve alcohol?		
When is the final head-count needed?		
What is your ratio of servers to guests?		
How do your servers dress for wedding receptions?		
What is your price range for a seated lunch/ buffet lunch?		
What is your price range for a seated/buffet dinner?		
How much gratuity is expected?		
What is your labor fee per employee?		
What is your cake-cutting fee?		
What is your bartending fee?		
What is your fee to clean-up after the reception?		
What is your payment/cancellation policy?		
Do you accept credit cards?		

CATERER COMPARISON CHART

POSSIBILITY 3	POSSIBILITY 4	POSSIBILITY 5

Menu Worksheet

HORS D'OEUVRES

_____
_____
_____

SALADS/APPETIZERS

_____
_____
_____

SOUPS

_____
_____
_____

MAIN ENTRÉE

_____
_____
_____

DESSERTS

_____
_____
_____

WEDDING CAKE

_____
_____
_____

MUSIC

Ceremony Music Comparison Chart

QUESTIONS	POSSIBILITY 1	POSSIBILITY 2
What is the name of the musician or band?		
What is your address?		
What is the name & phone number of my contact person?		
How many years of professional experience do you have?		
What percentage of your business is dedicated to weddings?		
Are you the person who will perform at my wedding?		
What instrument(s) do you play?		
What type of music do you specialize in?		
What are your hourly fees?		
What is the cost of a soloist?		
What is the cost of a duet?		
What is the cost of a trio?		
What is the cost of a quartet?		
How would you dress for my wedding?		
Do you have liability insurance?		
Do you have a cordless microphone?		
What is your payment/cancellation policy?		

Ceremony Music Comparison Chart

POSSIBILITY 3	POSSIBILITY 4	POSSIBILITY 5

Reception Music Comparison Chart

QUESTIONS	POSSIBILITY 1	POSSIBILITY 2
What is the name of the musician? Band? DJ?		
What is your address?		
What is the name & phone number of my contact person?		
How many years of professional experience do you have?		
What percentage of your business is dedicated to wedding receptions?		
How many people are in your band?		
What type of music do you specialize in?		
What type of sound system do you have?		
Can you act as a master of ceremonies? How do you dress?		
Can you provide a light show?		
Do you have a cordless microphone?		
How many breaks do you take? How long are they?		
Do you play recorded music during breaks?		
Do you have liability insurance?		
What are your fees for a 4-hour reception?		
What is your cost for each additional hour?		
What is your payment/cancellation policy?		

RECEPTION MUSIC COMPARISON CHART

POSSIBILITY 3	POSSIBILITY 4	POSSIBILITY 5

RECEPTION MUSIC SELECTIONS

(Make a copy of this form and give it to your musicians).

WHEN	SELECTION	SONGWRITER	PLAYED BY
Receiving Line			
During Hors D'Oeuvres			
During Dinner			
During Dinner			
First Dance			
Second Dance			
Third Dance			
Bouquet Toss			
Garter Removal			
Garter Toss			
Cutting of the Cake			
Couple Leaving			
Other			

BAKERY

Bakery Comparison Chart

QUESTIONS	POSSIBILITY 1	POSSIBILITY 2
What is the name of the bakery?		
What is the address of the bakery?		
What is the name & phone number of my contact person?		
How many years have you been making wedding cakes?		
What are your wedding cake specialties?		
Do you offer free tasting of your wedding cakes?		
Do you freeze your wedding cakes?		
How far in advance should I order my cake?		
Can you make a groom's cake?		
Do you lend, rent or sell cake knives?		
What is the cost per serving of my desired cake?		
What is your cake pillar and plate rental fee, if any?		
Is this fee refundable upon the return of these items?		
When must these items be returned?		
What is your cake delivery and set-up fee?		
What is your payment policy?		
What is your cancellation policy?		

BAKERY COMPARISON CHART

POSSIBILITY 3	POSSIBILITY 4	POSSIBILITY 5

Personal Notes

FLOWERS

Florists Comparison Chart

QUESTIONS	POSSIBILITY 1	POSSIBILITY 2
What is the name of the florist?		
What is the address of the florist?		
What is the name & phone number of my contact person?		
How many years of professional floral experience do you have?		
What percentage of your business is dedicated to weddings?		
Do you have access to out-of-season flowers?		
Will you visit my wedding sites to make floral recommendations?		
Can you preserve my bridal bouquet?		
Do you rent vases and candleholders?		
Can you provide silk flowers?		
What is your cost of a bridal bouquet made of a dozen white roses?		
What is your cost of a boutonniere made of a single white rose?		
What is your cost of a corsage made with two gardenias?		
Do you have liability insurance? fee? Do you accept credit cards?		
What are your delivery/set-up fees?		
What is your payment/cancellation policy?		
What are your business hours?		

FLORISTS COMPARISON CHART

POSSIBILITY 3	POSSIBILITY 4	POSSIBILITY 5

Bouquets and Flowers

BRIDE'S BOUQUET

COLOR SCHEME

_____

STYLE

_____

FLOWERS

_____

_____

_____

GREENERY

_____

OTHER (Ribbons, Etc.)

_____

MAID OF HONOR'S BOUQUET

COLOR SCHEME

_____

STYLE

_____

FLOWERS

_____

_____

_____

GREENERY

_____

OTHER (Ribbons, Etc.)

_____

BOUQUETS AND FLOWERS (CONT.)

BRIDESMAIDS' BOUQUETS

COLOR SCHEME   _____

STYLE   _____

FLOWERS   _____

                 _____

                 _____

GREENERY   _____

OTHER (Ribbons, Etc.) _____

FLOWER GIRL'S BOUQUET

COLOR SCHEME   _____

STYLE   _____

FLOWERS   _____

                 _____

                 _____

GREENERY   _____

OTHER (Ribbons, Etc.) _____

Bouquets and Flowers (Cont.)

GROOM'S BOUTONNIERE _____

_____

USHERS AND OTHER BOUTONNIERES _____

_____

MOTHER OF THE BRIDE CORSAGE _____

_____

MOTHER OF THE GROOM CORSAGE _____

_____

ALTAR OR CHUPPAH _____

_____

STEPS TO ALTAR OR CHUPPAH _____

_____

PEWS _____

_____

ENTRANCE TO THE CEREMONY _____

_____

*B*OUQUETS AND *F*LOWERS (CONT.)

ENTRANCE TO RECEPTION _____

_____

RECEIVING LINE _____

_____

HEAD TABLE _____

_____

PARENTS' TABLE _____

_____

GUEST TABLES _____

_____

CAKE TABLE _____

_____

SERVING TABLES (BUFFET, DESSERT) _____

_____

GIFT TABLE _____

_____

Flowers and their Seasons

Flower	Winter	Spring	Summer	Fall
Allium		X	X	
Alstroemeria	X	X	X	X
Amaryllis	X		X	
Anemone	X	X		X
Aster	X	X	X	X
Baby's Breath	X	X	X	X
Bachelor's Button	X	X	X	X
Billy Buttons		X	X	
Bird of Paradise	X	X	X	X
Bouvardia	X	X	X	X
Calla Lily	X	X	X	X
Carnation	X	X	X	X
Celosia		X	X	
Chrysanthemum	X	X	X	X
Daffodils		X		
Dahlia			X	X
Delphinium			X	X
Eucalyptus	X	X	X	X
Freesia	X	X	X	X
Gardenia	X	X	X	X
Gerbera	X	X	X	X
Gladiolus	X	X	X	X
Iris	X	X	X	X
Liatris		X	X	X
Lily	X	X	X	X

FLOWERS AND THEIR SEASONS

Flower	Winter	Spring	Summer	Fall
Lily of the Valley		x		
Lisianthus		x	x	x
Narcissus	x	x		x
Nerine	x	x	x	x
Orchid (Cattleya)	x	x	x	x
Orchid (Cymbidium)	x	x	x	x
Peony		x		
Pincushion			x	
Protea	x			x
Queen Anne's Lace			x	
Ranunculus		x		
Rose	x	x	x	x
Saponaria			x	
Snapdragon		x	x	x
Speedwell			x	
Star of Bethlehem	x			x
Statice	x	x	x	x
Stephanotis	x	x	x	x
Stock	x	x	x	x
Sunflower		x	x	
Sweet Pea		x		
Tuberose			x	x
Tulip	x	x		
Waxflower	x	x		

Personal Notes

_____

_____

_____

_____

_____

_____

_____

_____

_____

_____

_____

_____

_____

_____

_____

_____

_____

_____

_____

_____

_____

_____

_____

_____

_____

_____

_____

_____

TRANSPORTATION

Transportation Comparison Chart

QUESTIONS	POSSIBILITY 1	POSSIBILITY 2
What is the name of the transportation service?		
What is the address of the transportation service?		
What is the name & phone number of my contact person?		
How many years have you been in business?		
How many vehicles do you have available?		
Can you provide a back-up vehicle in case of an emergency?		
What types of vehicles are available?		
What are the various sizes of vehicles available?		
How old are the vehicles?		
How many drivers are available?		
Can you show me photos of your drivers?		
How do your drivers dress for weddings?		
Do you have liability insurance?		
What is the minimum amount of time required to rent a vehicle?		
What is the cost per hour? Two hours? Three hours?		
How much gratuity is expected?		
What is your payment/cancellation policy?		

TRANSPORTATION COMPARISON CHART

POSSIBILITY 3	POSSIBILITY 4	POSSIBILITY 5

Wedding Day Transportation

TO CEREMONY SITE

Name	Pickup Time	Pickup Location	Vehicle/Driver
Bride			
Groom			
Bride's Parents			
Groom's Parents			
Bridesmaids			
Ushers			
Other Guests			
Other Guests			

TO RECEPTION SITE

Name	Pickup Time	Pickup Location	Vehicle/Driver
Bride & Groom			
Bride's Parents			
Groom's Parents			
Bridesmaids			
Ushers			
Other Guests			

RENTAL ITEMS

Rental Supplier Comparison Chart

QUESTIONS	POSSIBILITY 1	POSSIBILITY 2
What is the name of the party rental supplier?		
What is the address of the party rental supplier?		
What is the name & phone number of my contact person?		
How many years have you been in business?		
What are your hours of operation?		
Do you have liability insurance?		
What is the cost per item needed?		
What is the cost of pick-up and delivery?		
What is the cost of setting up the items rented?		
When would the items be delivered?		
When would the items be picked up after the event?		
What is your payment policy?		
What is your cancellation policy?		

RENTAL SUPPLIER COMPARISON CHART

POSSIBILITY 3	POSSIBILITY 4	POSSIBILITY 5

Ceremony Equipment Checklist

Rental Supplier_____   Contact Person _____

Address _____

Phone Number _____   Hours _____

Payment Policy _____

Cancellation Policy _____

Delivery Time _____   Tear Down Time _____

Setup Time _____   Pickup Time _____

QTY.	ITEM	DESCRIPTION	PRICE	TOTAL
_____	Arch/Altar	_____	_____	_____
_____	Canopy (Chuppah)	_____	_____	_____
_____	Backdrops	_____	_____	_____
_____	Floor Candelabra	_____	_____	_____
_____	Candles	_____	_____	_____
_____	Candlelighters	_____	_____	_____
_____	Kneeling Bench	_____	_____	_____
_____	Aisle Stanchions	_____	_____	_____
_____	Aisle Runners	_____	_____	_____
_____	Guest Book Stand	_____	_____	_____
_____	Gift Table	_____	_____	_____
_____	Chairs	_____	_____	_____
_____	Audio Equipment	_____	_____	_____
_____	Lighting	_____	_____	_____
_____	Heating/Cooling	_____	_____	_____
_____	Umbrellas/Tents	_____	_____	_____
_____	Bug Eliminator	_____	_____	_____
_____	Coat/Hat Rack	_____	_____	_____
_____	Garbage Cans	_____	_____	_____

RECEPTION EQUIPMENT CHECKLIST

Rental Supplier _____ Contact Person _____

Address _____

Phone Number _____ Hours _____

Payment Policy _____

Cancellation Policy _____

Delivery Time _____ Tear Down Time _____

Setup Time _____ Pickup Time _____

QTY.	ITEM	DESCRIPTION	PRICE	TOTAL
_____	Audio Equipment	_____	_____	_____
_____	Cake Table	_____	_____	_____
_____	Candelabras/Candles	_____	_____	_____
_____	Canopies	_____	_____	_____
_____	Coat/Hat Rack	_____	_____	_____
_____	Dance Floor	_____	_____	_____
_____	Bug Eliminator	_____	_____	_____
_____	Garbage Cans	_____	_____	_____
_____	Gift Table	_____	_____	_____
_____	Guest Tables	_____	_____	_____
_____	Heating/Cooling	_____	_____	_____
_____	High/Booster Chairs	_____	_____	_____
_____	Lighting	_____	_____	_____
_____	Mirror Disk Ball	_____	_____	_____
_____	Place Card Table	_____	_____	_____
_____	Tents	_____	_____	_____
_____	Umbrellas	_____	_____	_____
_____	Visual Equipment	_____	_____	_____
_____	Wheelchair Ramp	_____	_____	_____

PERSONAL NOTES

MISCELLANEOUS

Wedding Consultants Comparison Chart

QUESTIONS	POSSIBILITY 1	POSSIBILITY 2
What is the name of the wedding consultant?		
What is the address of the wedding consultant?		
What is the name & phone number of my contact person?		
How many years of professional experience do you have?		
How many consultants are in your company?		
Are you a member of the Association of Bridal Consultants?		
What services do you provide?		
What are your hourly fees?		
What is your fee for complete wedding planning?		
What is your fee to oversee the rehearsal and wedding day?		
What is your payment policy?		
What is your cancellation policy?		
Do you have liability insurance?		

WEDDING CONSULTANTS COMPARISON CHART

POSSIBILITY 3	POSSIBILITY 4	POSSIBILITY 5

Consultant's Information Form

(Make a copy of this form and give it to your wedding consultant)

THE WEDDING OF _____ & _____

Ceremony Site _____ **Phone No.** _____

Ceremony Address _____

Reception Site _____ **Phone No.** _____

Reception Address _____

Ceremony Services	Contact Person	Arrival Time	Departure Time	Phone
Florist				
Musicians				
Officiant				
Photographer				
Rental Supplier				
Site Coordinator				
Soloist				
Transportation				
Videographer				
Other				

Reception Services	Contact Person	Arrival Time	Departure Time	Phone
Baker				
Bartender				
Caterer				
Florist				
Gift Attendant				
Guest Book Attendant				
Musicians				
Rental Supplier				
Site Coordinator				
Transportation				
Valet Service				
Other				

*N*AME & *A*DDRESS *C*HANGE *F*ORM

To Whom it May Concern:

This is to inform you of my recent marriage and to request a change of name and/or address. The following information will be effective as of _____

My account/policy number is: _____

Under the name of: _____

PREVIOUS INFORMATION

Husband's Name _____   Phone No. _____

Previous Address: _____

Wife's Maiden Name _____   Phone No. _____

Previous Address: _____

PRESENT/FUTURE INFORMATION

Husband's Name _____   Phone No. _____

Wife's Name _____   Phone No. _____

New Address: _____

SPECIAL INSTRUCTIONS

- ☐ Change name
- ☐ Change address/phone
- ☐ Add spouse's name
- ☐ Send necessary forms to include my spouse on my policy/account
- ☐ We plan to continue service
- ☐ We plan to discontinue service after _____

If you have any questions, please feel free to contact us at (   ) _____

Husband's Signature _____

Wife's Signature _____

Change Of Address Worksheet

Company	Account or Policy No.	Phone or Address	Done
Auto Insurance	_____	_____	____
Auto Registration	_____	_____	____
Bank Accounts	_____	_____	____
	_____	_____	____
	_____	_____	____
	_____	_____	____
Credit Cards	_____	_____	____
	_____	_____	____
	_____	_____	____
	_____	_____	____
	_____	_____	____
Dentist	_____	_____	____
	_____	_____	____
Doctors	_____	_____	____
	_____	_____	____
	_____	_____	____
Driver's License	_____	_____	____
Employee Records	_____	_____	____
Insurance: Dental	_____	_____	____
Insurance: Disability	_____	_____	____
Insurance: Homeowner's	_____	_____	____
Insurance: Life	_____	_____	____
Insurance: Renter's	_____	_____	____
Insurance: Other	_____	_____	____
IRA Accounts	_____	_____	____
	_____	_____	____
Leases	_____	_____	____
	_____	_____	____
	_____	_____	____
Loan Companies	_____	_____	____
	_____	_____	____
	_____	_____	____

CHANGE OF ADDRESS WORKSHEET
(CONT.)

Company	Account or Policy No.	Phone or Address	Done
Magazines			
Memberships			
Mortgage			
Newspaper			
Passport			
Pensions			
Post Office			
Property Title			
Retirement Accounts			
Safe Deposit Box			
School Records			
Social Security			
Stock Broker			
Subscriptions			
Taxes			
Telephone Co.			
Utilities			
Voters Registration			
Will/Trust			
Other			

Personal Notes

TIMELINES

Wedding Party Timeline

(Sample)

This is a sample wedding party timeline. To develop your own, use the form on page 156. Use the extra space in the description column to write additional information such as addresses or any other comments that will help members of your wedding party understand what their roles are. Once you have created your own timeline, make a copy and give one to each member of your wedding party.

TIME	DESCRIPTION	BRIDE	BRIDE'S MOTHER	BRIDE'S FATHER	MAID OF HONOR	BRIDE'S MAIDS	BRIDE'S FAMILY	GROOM	GROOM'S MOTHER	GROOM'S FATHER	BEST MAN	USHERS	GROOM'S FAMILY	FLOWER GIRL	RING BEARER
2:00 PM	Manicurist Appointment:	✓	✓		✓	✓									
2:30 PM	Hair/Makeup Appointment:	✓	✓		✓	✓									
4:15 PM	Arrive at Dressing Site:	✓	✓		✓	✓									
4:30 PM	Arrive at Dressing Site:							✓			✓	✓			
4:45 PM	Pre-Ceremony Photos:							✓	✓	✓	✓	✓	✓		
5:15 PM	Arrive at Ceremony Site:							✓	✓	✓	✓	✓	✓		
5:15 PM	Pre-Ceremony Photos:	✓	✓	✓	✓	✓	✓								
5:20 PM	Give Officiant Marriage License & Fee										✓				
5:20 PM	Ushers receive seating chart											✓			
5:30 PM	Ushers hand out wedding program as guests arrive											✓			
5:30 PM	Arrive at ceremony site:													✓	✓
5:30 PM	Guest book attendant asks guests to sign in:														
5:30 PM	Prelude Music Begins:														
5:35 PM	Begin Seating Guests:											✓			
5:45 PM	Arrive at ceremony site:	✓	✓	✓	✓	✓	✓								
5:45 PM	Honored Guests are Seated:											✓			
5:50 PM	Groom's Parents are Seated								✓	✓		✓			
5:55 PM	Bride's Mother is Seated		✓									✓			
5:55 PM	Attendants line up and get ready for Procession				✓	✓						✓		✓	✓
5:56 PM	Bride's father takes his place next to Bride	✓		✓											
5:57 PM	Aisle Runner is rolled down the aisle											✓			
5:58 PM	Officiant, Groom, and Best Man enter from:							✓			✓				
6:00 PM	Processional music begins:														

$\mathcal{W}$EDDING $\mathcal{P}$ARTY $\mathcal{T}$IMELINE

(Sample)

TIME	DESCRIPTION	BRIDE	BRIDE'S MOTHER	BRIDE'S FATHER	MAID OF HONOR	BRIDE'S MAIDS	BRIDE'S FAMILY	GROOM	GROOM'S MOTHER	GROOM'S FATHER	BEST MAN	USHERS	GROOM'S FAMILY	FLOWER GIRL	RING BEARER
6:00 PM	Groom's Mother Stands up								✓						
6:01 PM	Ushers enter from:											✓			
6:02 PM	Bridesmaids, Maid of Honor, RB, FG, Bride & Father march up aisle	✓		✓	✓	✓								✓	✓
6:20 PM	Bride/Groom, FG/RB, Maid of Honor/Best Man march down aisle	✓			✓			✓			✓			✓	✓
6:22 PM	Mother/Father of Bride, Mother/Father of Groom march down aisle		✓	✓					✓	✓					
6:25 PM	Signing of Marriage Certificate:	✓			✓			✓			✓				
6:30 PM	Post ceremony photos taken:	✓	✓	✓	✓	✓	✓	✓	✓	✓	✓	✓	✓	✓	✓
6:30 PM	Cocktails and Hors D'oeuvres served:														
6:30 PM	Gift attendant watches over gifts as guests arrive:														
7:15 PM	Receiving Line is formed, or Band/DJ announces entrance of Bride &	✓						✓							
7:45 PM	Guests are seated & meal is served														
8:30 PM	Toasts										✓				
8:40 PM	First Dance	✓						✓							
8:45 PM	Traditional Dances:	✓	✓	✓				✓	✓	✓					
9:00 PM	Open dance floor for all guests														
9:30 PM	Bride & groom toast eachother before cutting cake	✓						✓							
9:40 PM	Cake-cutting ceremony	✓						✓							
10:00 PM	Bride tosses bouquet to single women	✓			✓	✓								✓	
10:10 PM	Groom takes garter from Bride's leg	✓						✓							
10:15 PM	Groom tosses garter to single men							✓			✓	✓			✓
10:20 PM	Man who caught garter puts on woman's leg who caught bouquet														
10:30 PM	Hand out rose petals, rice, or birdseed to toss over bride & groom as they														
10:45 PM	Grand Exit by Bride & Groom	✓						✓							

Wedding Party Timeline

(Create your own timeline using this form, make copies, and give one to each member of your wedding party).

TIME	DESCRIPTION	BRIDE	BRIDE'S MOTHER	BRIDE'S FATHER	MAID OF HONOR	BRIDE'S MAIDS	BRIDE'S FAMILY	GROOM	GROOM'S MOTHER	GROOM'S FATHER	BEST MAN	USHERS	GROOM'S FAMILY	FLOWER GIRL	RING BEARER

WEDDING PARTY TIMELINE

(Continuation)

TIME	DESCRIPTION	BRIDE	BRIDE'S MOTHER	BRIDE'S FATHER	MAID OF HONOR	BRIDE'S MAIDS	BRIDE'S FAMILY	GROOM	GROOM'S MOTHER	GROOM'S FATHER	BEST MAN	USHERS	GROOM'S FAMILY	FLOWER GIRL	RING BEARER

Service Provider Timeline

(Sample)

This is a sample of a service provider timeline. To develop your own, use the form on page 160. Use the extra space in the description column to write additional information such as addresses or any other comments that will help your service providers understand what their roles are and where they should be throughout the day. Once you have created your own timeline, make a copy and give one to each of your service providers.

TIME	DESCRIPTION	BAKERY	CATERER	CEREM. MUSICIAN	OFFICIANT	OTHER	FLORIST	HAIR DRESSER	LIMOUSINE	MAKEUP ARTIST	MANICURIST	PARTY RENTALS	PHOTOGRAPHER	RECEP. MUSICIANS	VIDEOGRAPHER
1:00 PM	Party rental supplier drops off supplies at ceremony site:											✓			
1:30 PM	Party rental supplier drops off supplies at reception site:											✓			
2:00 PM	Manicurist meets bride at:										✓				
2:30 PM	Makeup artist meets bride at:									✓					
3:00 PM	Hair dresser meets bride at:							✓							
4:00 PM	Limousine picks up bridal party at:								✓						
4:15 PM	Caterer begins setting up:		✓												
4:30 PM	Florist arrives at ceremony site:						✓								
4:40 PM	Baker delivers cake to reception site:	✓													
4:45 PM	Florist arrives at reception site:						✓								
4:45 PM	Pre-ceremony photos of groom's family at:												✓		
5:00 PM	Videographer arrives at ceremony site:														✓
5:15 PM	Pre-ceremony photos of bride's family at:												✓		
5:20 PM	Ceremony site decorations are completed (guest book table, flowers, etc)					✓	✓								
5:30 PM	Prelude music begins:			✓											
5:45 PM	Reception site decorations completed (gift table, place cards, flowers, etc)	✓				✓	✓								
5:58 PM	Officiant enters from:				✓										
6:00 PM	Processional music begins:			✓											
6:15 PM	Caterer finishes setting up:		✓												
6:25 PM	Bride & Groom sign marriage certificate				✓								✓		✓
6:30 PM	Post-ceremony photos of wedding party at:												✓		
6:30 PM	Cocktails & Hors D'oeuvres served:		✓												
6:30 PM	Band/DJ starts playing:													✓	

SERVICE PROVIDER TIMELINE

(Sample)

TIME	DESCRIPTION	BAKERY	CATERER	CEREM. MUSICIAN	OFFICIANT	OTHER	FLORIST	HAIR DRESSER	LIMOUSINE	MAKEUP ARTIST	MANICURIST	PARTY RENTALS	PHOTOGRAPHER	RECEP. MUSICIANS	VIDEOGRAPHER
6:30 PM	Move guest book & gifts to reception site					✓									
6:30 PM	Ceremony music ends			✓											
6:45 AM	Move arch/urns/flowers to reception site					✓									
7:00 PM	Limousine picks up Bride & Groom at ceremony site:								✓						
7:15 PM	Band/DJ announces entrance of Bride & Groom													✓	
7:45 PM	Meal is served		✓												
8:10 PM	Band/DJ announces champagne will be served for toasts													✓	
8:15 PM	Champagne is served for toasts		✓												
8:30 PM	Band/DJ announces toast by Best Man													✓	
8:40 PM	Band/DJ announces first dance													✓	
9:00 PM	Transport gifts to:					✓									
9:30 PM	Band/DJ announces cake-cutting ceremony													✓	
10:30 PM	Transport top tier of cake & flowers to:					✓									
10:40 PM	Transport rental items that need to be returned to:					✓									
10:45 PM	Limousine picks up Bride & Groom at reception site:								✓						
11:00 PM	Videographer departs														✓
11:00 PM	Photographer departs												✓		
11:00 PM	Wedding consultant departs					✓									
11:30 PM	Band/DJ stops playing													✓	
11:45 PM	Party rental supplier picks up supplies at ceremony/reception sites											✓			

Service Provider Timeline

(Create your own timeline using this form, make copies, and give one to each of your service providers).

TIME	DESCRIPTION	BAKERY	CATERER	CEREM. MUSICIAN	OFFICIANT	OTHER	FLORIST	HAIR DRESSER	LIMOUSINE	MAKEUP ARTIST	MANICURIST	PARTY RENTALS	PHOTOGRAPHER	RECEP. MUSICIANS	VIDEOGRAPHER

SERVICE PROVIDER TIMELINE

(Continuation)

TIME	DESCRIPTION	BAKERY	CATERER	CEREM. MUSICIAN	OFFICIANT	OTHER	FLORIST	HAIR DRESSER	LIMOUSINE	MAKEUP ARTIST	MANICURIST	PARTY RENTALS	PHOTOGRAPHER	RECEP. MUSICIANS	VIDEOGRAPHER

PERSONAL NOTES

_____
_____
_____
_____
_____
_____
_____
_____
_____
_____
_____
_____
_____
_____
_____
_____
_____
_____
_____
_____
_____
_____
_____
_____
_____
_____
_____
_____
_____
_____
_____

Wedding Party Responsibilities

Wedding Party Responsibilities

Each member of your wedding party has his/her own individual duties and responsibilities. The following is a list of the most important duties for each member of your wedding party.

The most convenient method for conveying this information to members of your wedding party is by purchasing a set of the *Wedding Party Responsibility Cards,* published by Wedding Solutions Publishing, Inc.

These cards are very attractive and contain all the information your wedding party needs to know to assure a smooth wedding: what to do, how to do it, when to do it, when to arrive, and much more. They also include financial responsibilities as well as the processional, recessional and altar line-up. These cards are available at most major bookstores. But you can purchase them directly from Wedding Solutions Publishing, Inc. by sending $6.95 plus $2.95 for shipping and handling to Wedding Solutions Publishing, Inc., 6347 Caminito Tenedor, San Diego, CA 92120.

Maid of Honor

- ◆ Helps bride select attire and address invitations.
- ◆ Plans bridal shower for bride.
- ◆ Arrives at dressing site 2 hours before ceremony to assist bride in dressing.
- ◆ Arrives dressed at ceremony site 1 hour before the wedding for photographs.
- ◆ Arranges the bride's veil and train before the processional and recessional.
- ◆ Holds bride's bouquet and groom's ring, if no ring bearer, during the ceremony.
- ◆ Witnesses the signing of the marriage license.
- ◆ Keeps bride on schedule.
- ◆ Dances with best man during the bridal party dance.
- ◆ Helps bride change into her going away clothes.
- ◆ Mails wedding announcements after the wedding.
- ◆ Returns bridal slip, if rented.

BEST MAN

- Responsible for organizing ushers' activities.
- Organizes bachelor party for groom.
- Drives groom to ceremony site and sees that he is properly dressed before the wedding.
- Arrives dressed at ceremony site 1 hour before the wedding for photographs.
- Brings marriage license to wedding.
- Pays the clergyman, musicians, photographer, and any other service providers the day of the wedding.
- Holds the bride's ring for the groom, if no ring bearer, until needed by officiant.
- Witnesses the signing of the marriage license.
- Drives newlyweds to reception if no hired driver.
- Offers first toast at reception, usually before dinner.
- Keeps groom on schedule.
- Dances with maid of honor during the bridal party dance.
- May drive couple to airport or honeymoon suite.
- Oversees return of tuxedo rentals for groom and ushers, on time and in good condition.

BRIDESMAIDS

- Assist maid/matron of honor in planning bridal shower.
- Assist bride with errands and addressing invitations.
- Participate in all pre-wedding parties.
- Arrive at dressing site 2 hours before ceremony.
- Arrive dressed at ceremony site 1 hour before the wedding for photographs.
- Walk behind ushers in order of height during the processional, either in pairs or in single file.
- Sit next to ushers at the head table.
- Dance with ushers and other important guests.
- Encourage single women to participate in the bouquet-tossing ceremony.

Ushers

- Help best man with bachelor party.
- Arrive dressed at ceremony site 1 hour before the wedding for photographs.
- Distribute wedding programs and maps to the reception as guests arrive.
- Seat guests at the ceremony as follows:
    - -- If female, offer the right arm.
    - -- If male, walk along his left side.
    - -- If couple, offer right arm to female; male follows a step or two behind.
    - -- Seat bride's guests in left pews.
    - -- Seat groom's guests in right pews.
    - -- Maintain equal number of guests in left and right pews, if possible.
    - -- If a group of guests arrive at the same time, seat the eldest woman first.
    - -- Just prior to the processional, escort groom's mother to her seat; then escort bride's mother to her seat.
- Two ushers may roll carpet down the aisle after both mothers are seated.
- If pew ribbons are used, two ushers may loosen them one row at a time after the ceremony.
- Direct guests to the reception site.
- Dance with bridesmaids and other important guests.

Bride's Mother

- Helps prepare guest list for bride and her family.
- Helps plan the wedding ceremony and reception.
- Helps bride select her bridal gown.
- Helps bride keep track of gifts received.
- Selects her own attire according to the formality and color of the wedding.
- Makes accommodations for bride's out of town guests.
- Arrives dressed at ceremony site 1 hour before the wedding for photographs.
- Is the last person to be seated right before the processional begins.
- Sits in the left front pew to the left of bride's father during the ceremony.
- May stand up to signal the start of the processional.
- Can witness the signing of the marriage license.
- Dances with the groom after the first dance.
- Acts as hostess at the reception.

BRIDE'S FATHER

- Helps prepare guest list for bride and her family.
- Selects attire that complements groom's attire.
- Rides to the ceremony with bride in limousine.
- Arrives dressed at ceremony site 1 hour before the wedding for photographs.
- After giving bride away, sits in the left front pew to the right of bride's mother. If divorced, sits in second or third row unless financing the wedding.
- When officiant asks, "Who gives this bride away?" answers, "Her mother and I do" or something similar.
- Can witness the signing of the marriage license.
- Dances with bride after first dance.
- Acts as host at the reception.

GROOM'S MOTHER

- Helps prepare guest list for groom and his family.
- Selects attire that complements mother of the bride's attire.
- Makes accommodations for groom's out-of-town guests.
- With groom's father, plans rehearsal dinner.
- Arrives dressed at ceremony site 1 hour before the wedding for photographs.
- May stand up to signal the start of the processional.
- Can witness the signing of the marriage license.

GROOM'S FATHER

- Helps prepare guest list for groom and his family.
- Selects attire that complements groom's attire.
- With groom's mother, plans rehearsal dinner.
- Offers toast to bride at rehearsal dinner.
- Arrives dressed at ceremony site 1 hour before the wedding for photographs.
- Can witness the signing of the marriage license.

Flower Girl

- Usually between the ages of four and eight.
- Attends rehearsal to practice but is not required to attend pre-wedding parties.
- Arrives dressed at ceremony site 45 minutes before the wedding for photos.
- Carries a basket filled with loose rose petals to strew along bride's path during processional, if allowed by ceremony site.
- If very young, may sit with her parents during ceremony.

Ring Bearer

- Usually between the ages of four and eight.
- Attends rehearsal to practice but is not required to attend pre-wedding parties.
- Arrives at ceremony site 45 minutes before the wedding for photographs.
- Carries a white pillow with rings attached.
- If younger than 7 years, carries artificial rings.
- If very young, may sit with his parents during ceremony.
- After ceremony, carries ring pillow upside down so artificial rings do not show.

WEDDING PARTY FORM

(Make a copy of this form and give it to your wedding consultant).

Parents	Home No.	Work No.	Responsibilities
Bride's Mother			
Bride's Father			
Groom's Mother			
Groom's Father			

Bride's Attendants	Home No.	Work No.	Responsibilities
Maid of Honor			
Matron of Honor			
Bridesmaid			
Bridesmaid			
Bridesmaid			
Bridesmaid			
Bridesmaid			
Bridesmaid			
Flower Girl			
Flower Girl			
Other			

Groom's Attendants	Home No.	Work No.	Responsibilities
Best Man			
Usher			
Usher			
Usher			
Usher			
Usher			
Usher			
Ring Bearer			
Ring Bearer			
Other			

$\mathcal{W}$HO $\mathcal{P}$AYS $\mathcal{F}$OR $\mathcal{W}$HAT

BRIDE AND/OR BRIDE'S FAMILY

- Engagement party
- Wedding consultant's fee
- Bridal gown, veil and accessories
- Wedding stationery, calligraphy and postage
- Wedding gift for bridal couple
- Groom's wedding ring
- Gifts for bridesmaids
- Bridesmaids' bouquets
- Pre-wedding parties and bridesmaids' luncheon
- Photography and videography
- Bride's medical exam and blood test
- Wedding guest book and other accessories
- Total cost of the ceremony, including location, flowers, music, rental items and ccessories
- Total cost of the reception, including location, flowers, music, rental items, accessories, food, beverages, cake, decorations, favors, etc.
- Transportation for bridal party to ceremony and reception
- Own attire and travel expenses

GROOM AND/OR GROOM'S FAMILY

- Own travel expenses and attire
- Rehearsal dinner
- Wedding gift for bridal couple
- Bride's wedding ring
- Gifts for groom's attendants
- Medical exam for groom including blood test
- Bride's bouquet and going away corsage
- Mothers' and grandmothers' corsages
- All boutonnieres
- Officiant's fee
- Marriage license
- Honeymoon expenses

ATTENDANTS

- Own attire except flowers
- Travel expenses
- Bridal shower paid for by maid of honor and bridesmaids
- Bachelor party paid for by best man and ushers

WEDDING

FORMATIONS

CHRISTIAN CEREMONY

ALTAR LINE UP

Bride's Pews   Groom's Pews

ABBREVIATIONS

B = Bride	GF = Groom's Father
G = Groom	GM = Groom's Mother
BM = Best Man	BMa = Bridesmaids
MH = Maid of Honor	U = Ushers
BF = Bride's Father	FG = Flower Girl
BMo = Bride's Mother	RB = Ring Bearer
	O = Officiant

CHRISTIAN CEREMONY

PROCESSIONAL   RECESSIONAL

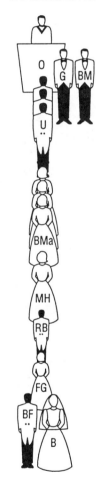
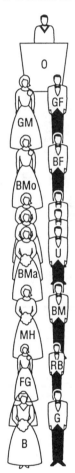

ABBREVIATIONS

B = Bride   GF = Groom's Father
G = Groom   GM = Groom's Mother
BM = Best Man   BMa = Bridesmaids
MH = Maid of Honor   U = Ushers
BF = Bride's Father   FG = Flower Girl
BMo = Bride's Mother   RB = Ring Bearer
                            O = Officiant

JEWISH CEREMONY

ALTAR LINE UP

Groom's Pews   Bride's Pews

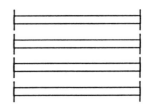

ABBREVIATIONS

B = Bride	GF = Groom's Father
G = Groom	GM = Groom's Mother
BM = Best Man	BMa = Bridesmaids
MH = Maid of Honor	U = Ushers
BF = Bride's Father	FG = Flower Girl
BMo = Bride's Mother	RB = Ring Bearer
	R = Rabbi

JEWISH CEREMONY

PROCESSIONAL   RECESSIONAL

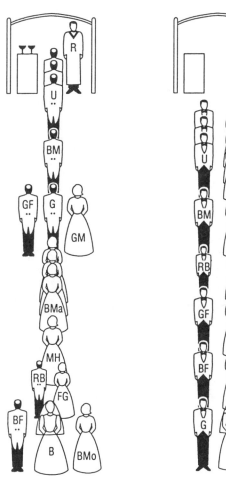

ABBREVIATIONS

B = Bride	GF = Groom's Father
G = Groom	GM = Groom's Mother
BM = Best Man	BMa = Bridesmaids
MH = Maid of Honor	U = Ushers
BF = Bride's Father	FG = Flower Girl
BMo = Bride's Mother	RB = Ring Bearer
	R = Rabbi

RECEIVING LINE

HEAD TABLE

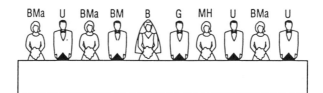

PARENTS' TABLE

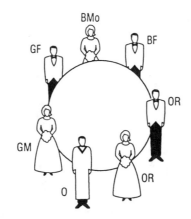

ABBREVIATIONS

B = Bride	GF = Groom's Father
G = Groom	GM = Groom's Mother
BM = Best Man	BMa = Bridesmaids
MH = Maid of Honor	U = Ushers
BF = Bride's Father	OR = Other Relatives
BMo = Bride's Mother	O = Officiant

THINGS TO BRING

$\mathcal{T}$HINGS $\mathcal{T}$O $\mathcal{B}$RING

$\mathcal{T}$O THE REHEARSAL

Bride's List:

- ❑ Wedding announcements (maid of honor to mail after wedding)
- ❑ Bridesmaids' gifts (if not already given)
- ❑ Camera and film
- ❑ Fake bouquet or ribbon bouquet from bridal shower
- ❑ Groom's gift (if not already given)
- ❑ Reception maps and wedding programs
- ❑ Rehearsal information and ceremony formations
- ❑ Flower girl basket and ring bearer pillow
- ❑ Seating diagrams for head table and parents' tables
- ❑ Wedding schedule of events/timeline
- ❑ Tape player with wedding music

Groom's List:

- ❑ Bride's gift (if not already given)
- ❑ Marriage license
- ❑ Ushers' gifts (if not already given)
- ❑ Service providers' fees to give to best man or wedding consultant so s/he can pay them at the wedding

TO THE CEREMONY

Bride's List:

- ❑ Aspirin/Alka Seltzer
- ❑ Bobby pins
- ❑ Breath spray/mints
- ❑ Bridal gown
- ❑ Bridal gown box
- ❑ Cake knife
- ❑ Change of clothes for going away
- ❑ Clear nail polish
- ❑ Deodorant
- ❑ Garter
- ❑ Gloves
- ❑ Groom's ring
- ❑ Guest book
- ❑ Hair brush
- ❑ Hair spray
- ❑ Head piece
- ❑ Iron
- ❑ Jewelry
- ❑ Kleenex
- ❑ Lint brush
- ❑ Luggage
- ❑ Make-up
- ❑ Mirror
- ❑ Nail polish
- ❑ Panty hose
- ❑ Passport
- ❑ Perfume
- ❑ Personal camera
- ❑ Plume pen for guest book
- ❑ Powder
- ❑ Purse
- ❑ Safety pins
- ❑ Scotch tape/masking tape
- ❑ Sewing kit
- ❑ Shoes
- ❑ Something old
- ❑ Something new

- ❑ Something borrowed
- ❑ Something blue
- ❑ Spot remover
- ❑ Straight pins
- ❑ Tampons or sanitary napkins
- ❑ Toasting goblets
- ❑ Toothbrush & paste

Groom's List:

- ❑ Airline tickets
- ❑ Announcements
- ❑ Aspirin/Alka Seltzer
- ❑ Breath spray/mints
- ❑ Bride's ring
- ❑ Change of clothes for going away
- ❑ Cologne
- ❑ Cuff Links
- ❑ Cummerbund
- ❑ Deodorant
- ❑ Hair comb
- ❑ Hair spray
- ❑ Kleenex
- ❑ Lint brush
- ❑ Luggage
- ❑ Neck tie
- ❑ Passport
- ❑ Shirt
- ❑ Shoes
- ❑ Socks
- ❑ Toothbrush & paste
- ❑ Tuxedo
- ❑ Underwear

THINGS TO DO

Things To Do

DONE BY
  ✓   (B = Bride, G = Groom)

THINGS TO DO

DONE BY
✓   (B = Bride, G = Groom)

THINGS TO DO

DONE BY
✓   (B = Bride, G = Groom)

EASY

HONEYMOON

PLANNER

$\mathcal{C}$HOOSING $\mathcal{Y}$OUR $\mathcal{D}$ESTINATION

Maybe your idea of a perfect honeymoon is ten days of resting in a beach chair and romantic strolls in the evening; but for your fiancé, it may be ten days of adventure and discovery. The choices for honeymoon vacations are as varied as the bride and groom themselves. Deciding together on a honeymoon destination is a wonderful opportunity to discover more about each other and negotiate a vacation that will leave both of you relaxed, fulfilled, and even more in love.

$\mathcal{C}$REATING A $\mathcal{W}$ISH $\mathcal{L}$IST

Together with your fiancé, complete the following wish list worksheet for your honeymoon destination. You should each check off your preferences even if both of you don't agree on them. There are many locations that provide a variety of activities. Remember, you don't need to spend every minute of your honeymoon together, but your honeymoon destination should be one that intrigues both of you.

While completing the worksheet, be as true to your interests as possible; don't concern yourself with finances and practicality at this point. This is your chance to let your mind wander! Think about what you would like to fill your days and nights with. This is the honeymoon of your dreams...

On the following worksheet, each of you separately should place a check mark next to the items or images on the wish list that appeal to you. After you have finished, highlight those items that both of you feel are important (the items that were checked by both of you).

Next, each of you should highlight, in a different colored marker or pen, 2-3 items in each category that you feel are very important to you individually (even though the other person may not have checked it.)

Your wish lists, after completing this exercise, will probably look like a list of *all* of the positive elements of *all* of your dream vacations combined. This is good; you should list as many things as you can think of. The more information you have, the better the suggestions your travel agent (or yourself if you'll be doing your own research) will be able to make.

Together, using this wish list, you will discover a honeymoon destination and match a honeymoon style that will fulfill your dreams. Happy planning!

	BRIDE √	GROOM √
Location:		
hot weather		
mild weather		
cold weather		
dry climate		
moist climate		
sand and beaches		
lakes/ponds		
wilderness/wooded areas		
mountains		
fields		
city streets		
small local town		
large metropolitan area		
popular tourist destination		
visiting among the locals		
nighttime weather conducive to outdoor activities		
nighttime weather conducive to indoor activities		
"modern" resources and service available		
"roughing it" on your own		
culture and customs you are familiar and comfortable with		
new cultures and customs you would like to get to know		
Accommodations:		
part of a larger resort community		
a stand alone building		
lodging amongst other fellow tourists		

	BRIDE ✓	GROOM ✓
lodging amongst couples only		
lodging amongst fellow newlyweds only		
lodging amongst locals		
large room or suite		
plush, highly decorated surroundings		
modestly sized room		
modest decor		
balcony		
private Jacuzzi in room		
room service		
chamber maid service		
laundry / dry cleaning service available		
laundry room available		
beauty salon on premises		
workout gym on premises		
gift shop on premises		
pool on premises		
poolside bar service		
sauna, hot tub on premises		
common gathering lounge for guests		
Meals:		
casual dining		
formal dining		
prepared by executive chefs		
prepared by yourself/grocery store		
variety of local and regional restaurants		
traditional "American" cuisine		
opportunity for picnics		
exotic, international menu		

	BRIDE ✓	GROOM ✓
entertainment while dining		
planned meal times		
dining based on your own schedule		
fast food restaurants		
vegetarian meals, special diet meals		
delis, diners		
Activities:		
sun bathing		
snorkeling		
diving		
swimming		
jet skiing		
water skiing		
fishing		
sailing		
snow skiing		
snow boarding		
hiking, rock climbing		
camping		
golf		
tennis		
aerobics		
site-seeing suggestions and guidance		
planned bus/guided tours		
ability to go off on your own		
historic tours		
art museums		
theater		
exploring family heritage		

	BRIDE ✓	GROOM ✓
Night Life:		
quiet strolls		
outdoor activities		
sitting and relaxing outdoors		
sitting and relaxing in front of a fireplace		
being alone with each other		
being out with the locals		
being out with other newlyweds		
discovering new cultures and forms of entertainment		
dancing		
visiting bars/pubs		
theater / shows		
gambling		
Other important elements:		

CREATING A BUDGET

You want your honeymoon to give you luxurious experiences and priceless memories. But you don't want to return from your vacation faced with debts and unnecessary feelings of guilt for not having stayed within a reasonable budget.

This should be the vacation of a lifetime. You can make this trip into anything your imagination allows. Pay attention to which experiences or details you would consider a "must have" and prioritize. As you work with your budget, stay focused on those top priority items and allow less "elaborate" solutions for lower priority items. If you stay true to your most important vacation objectives, the minor sacrifices along the way will barely be noticed.

Perhaps, at this point, you don't know how many days your honeymoon will last. Often, the number of days you'll vacation depends on the type of honeymoon you choose. If you (and your travel agent) are designing your own honeymoon, the typical cost-per-day will most likely determine your length of stay. If you opt for a cruise or another type of prearranged vacation, your length of stay will probably be dependent upon the designated length of the travel package. By determining a basic, overall budget at the start, you will know what your limits are.

Yes, this is a very romantic time... but try to remain realistic! Once you have an idea of your spending limits, your choices will be much easier to make.

Don't be discouraged if you're unable to spend an infinite amount of money on this trip. Very few couples are able to live life so carefree. You can still experience a honeymoon that will leave you filled with those priceless memories... it's all in the planning!

The following budget worksheets will help guide you in creating your honeymoon budget. You may want to make copies of this worksheet so that you can create several budget plans. Keep trying different variations until you are satisfied with how your expenses will be allocated. When comparing your potential honeymoon options, you'll find that laying out a simple budget is an effective, and essential, tool for making decisions.

General Budget

**Amount from Wedding Budget set aside
for Honeymoon:** $_____

**Amount Groom is able to contribute from
current funds/savings:** $_____

**Amount Bride is able to contribute from
current funds/savings:** $_____

**Amount to be saved/acquired by Groom
from now until the honeymoon date:** $_____
(monthly contributions, part-time job, gifts, bonuses)

**Amount to be saved/acquired by Bride
from now until the honeymoon date:** $_____
(monthly contributions, part-time job, gifts, bonuses)

**"GENERAL BUDGET"
TOTAL AMOUNT:**

$_____

DETAILED BUDGET

BEFORE THE HONEYMOON:

Special honeymoon clothing purchases: $_____

Bride's trousseau (honeymoon lingerie): $_____

Sundries: $_____
(HELPFUL HINT: Make a list of what you already have
and what you need to purchase. You can then use these
lists as part of your Packing List. See *Packing Checklist.*)

Film, disposable cameras, extra camera batteries: $_____

Maps, guide books, travel magazines: $_____

**Foreign language books and tapes,
translation dictionary:** $_____

Passport photos, application fees: $_____
(See *International Travel*)

Medical exam, inoculations: $_____
(See *International Travel*)

Other items: $_____

_____

_____

_____

BEFORE THE HONEYMOON
TOTAL AMOUNT:

$_____

During the honeymoon:

TRANSPORTATION:

Airplane tickets: $_____

Shuttle or cab (to and from airport): $_____

Car rental, Gasoline, tolls: $_____

Taxis, buses, other public transportation: $_____

> ### *TRANSPORTATION*
> ### TOTAL AMOUNT:
>
> $_____

ACCOMMODATIONS:

Hotel/resort room (total for entire stay): $_____

Room service: $_____

Miscellaneous "hidden costs": $_____
Phone use, room taxes and surcharges, chambermaid
and room service tips (see *Tipping Guide*),
in-room liquor bar and snacks.

> ### *ACCOMMODATIONS*
> ### TOTAL AMOUNT:
>
> $_____

MEALS:
(NOTE: Don't forget to include the cost of drinks and gratuities in your meal estimates.)

Breakfast: $_____ *per meal* x _____ *# days* = $_____

Lunch: $_____ *per meal* x _____ *# days* = $_____

Casual
Dinners: $_____ *per meal* x _____ *# days* = $_____

Formal
Dinners: $_____ *per meal* x _____ *# days* = $_____

Picnics, $_____ *per meal* x _____ *# days* = $_____
Snacks,Temptations:

```
+--------------------------------------+
|            MEALS                     |
|         TOTAL AMOUNT:                |
|                                      |
|        $_____     |
+--------------------------------------+
```

ENTERTAINMENT:

Sport and activity lessons
(tennis, golf, ballroom dancing, etc.): $_____

Day excursions and tours
(boat tours, diving, snorkeling, bus/guided tours, etc.): $_____

Shows, theater: $_____

Lounges, nightclubs, discos:
(don't forget to include the cost of drinks and bar gratuities) $_____

Museum fees: $_____

Pampering
(massages, spa treatments, hairdresser, etc.): $_____

```
+--------------------------------------+
|         ENTERTAINMENT                |
|         TOTAL AMOUNT:                |
|                                      |
|        $_____     |
+--------------------------------------+
```

MISCELLANEOUS:

Souvenirs for yourselves: $ _____

Souvenirs and gifts for family and friends: $ _____

Postcards (including cost of stamps): $ _____

Newspapers and magazines: $ _____

Additional film, replacement sundries, other: $ _____

```
MISCELLANEOUS
TOTAL AMOUNT:

$ _____
```

AFTER THE HONEYMOON:

Film developing costs: $ _____

Photo Albums: $ _____

```
AFTER THE HONEYMOON
TOTAL AMOUNT:

$ _____
```

For All-Inclusive Resorts/Cruises and Travel Packages only:

Fill in the entire budget form above (simply put a "$0.00" on items to be included in the total package price), then list the total inclusive package price on the line below. Don't forget to include taxes and surcharges.

Inclusive Package Price: $ _____

```
DETAILED BUDGET TOTAL AMOUNT:

$ _____
```

Things To Pack

Travelers' First Aid Kit

Consider the differences in the climates of where you live now and where you'll be visiting. Also consider the air conditions of airplanes, trains and boats. Bring along items that will help in the transition and keep you feeling as comfortable as possible.

- ❏ *Aspirin*
- ❏ *Antacid tablets*
- ❏ *Diarrhea medication*
- ❏ *Cold remedies/ sinus decongestant*
- ❏ *Throat lozenges*
- ❏ *Antiseptic Lotion*
- ❏ *Band-Aids*
- ❏ *Moleskin for blisters*
- ❏ *Breath mints*
- ❏ *Chapstick*
- ❏ *Insect Repellent, Insect Bite Medication*
- ❏ *Sunblock and Sunburn Relief Lotion*
- ❏ *Dry Skin Lotion/Hand Cream*
- ❏ *Eye Drops or Eye Lubricant*
- ❏ *Saline nasal spray, moisturizing nasal spray*
- ❏ *Vitamins*
- ❏ *Prescription drugs*
  NOTE: These should be kept in their original pharmacy containers which provide both drug and doctor information. Be sure to note the drug's generic name. You will want to pack these in your carry on baggage in case the bags you've checked become lost or delayed.
- ❏ *Condoms or prescription birth control*
- ❏ *Physicians' names, addresses, and telephone numbers*
- ❏ *Health Insurance phone numbers*
  NOTE: Be sure to contact your provider to find out about coverage while traveling in the U.S. and abroad.
- ❏ *Names and phone numbers of people to contact in case of an emergency*

CARRY ON BAGGAGE:

- ❑ Travelers' First Aid Kit (see previous section)
- ❑ Wallet (credit cards, traveler's checks)
- ❑ Jewelry and other sentimental and valuable items that you feel you *must* bring
- ❑ Identification (Passport, Driver's License or Photo ID)
- ❑ Photocopies of the following Important Documents:
    - ❑ Hotel/resort street address, phone number, written confirmation of arrangements and reservations
    - ❑ Complete travel itinerary
    - ❑ Airline tickets
    - ❑ Name, address and phone number of emergency contact person(s) back home
    - ❑ Medicine prescriptions (including generic names) and eyeglass prescription information (or an extra pair); list of food and drug allergies
    - ❑ Phone numbers (including after-hour emergency phone numbers) for health insurance company and personal physicians
- ❑ Copy of your packing list. This will help you while packing up at the end of your trip. It will also be invaluable if a piece of your luggage gets lost, as you will know the contents that are missing.
- ❑ List of your travelers checks' serial numbers and 24 hour phone number for reporting loss or theft
- ❑ Phone numbers to the local U.S. embassy or consulate
- ❑ Any "essential" toiletries and one complete casual outfit in case checked baggage is delayed or lost
- ❑ Foreign language dictionary or translator
- ❑ Camera with film loaded
- ❑ Maps
- ❑ Small bills/change (in U.S. dollars and in the appropriate foreign currency) for tipping
- ❑ Currency converter chart or pocket calculator
- ❑ Reading material
- ❑ Eyeglasses
- ❑ Contact lenses
- ❑ Contact lens cleaner

❏   Sunglasses

❏   Kleenex, gum, breath mints, and any over-the-counter medicine to ease travel discomfort

❏   Inflatable neck pillow (for lengthy, sit down travels)

❏   Address book and thank you notes (in case you have lots of traveling time)

❏   This Book

❏   Your Budget Sheet

❏   **Other items to carry-on ...**

❏   _____

❏   _____

❏   _____

❏   _____

CHECKED BAGGAGE:

Clothing:

❏   *Casual wear*
(Consider the total number of each casual outfit item that you will need)

    ❏   shorts

    ❏   pants

    ❏   tops

    ❏   jackets/sweaters

    ❏   sweatshirts/sweatsuits

    ❏   belts

    ❏   socks

    ❏   underwear/panties & bras

    ❏   walking shoes/sandals/loafers

    ❏   _____

    ❏   _____

❏   *Athletic wear*
(Consider the total number of each sporting outfit item that you will need)

    ❏   shorts

    ❏   sweatpants

- ❑ tops
- ❑ sweatshirts/jackets
- ❑ swim suits, swim suit cover-up
- ❑ aerobic activity outfit
- ❑ athletic equipment
- ❑ hats
- ❑ socks
- ❑ underwear/panties & exercise bras
- ❑ tennis/athletic shoes
- ❑ _____
- ❑ _____

❑ *Evening wear*
(Consider the total number of each evening outfit item that you will need)
- ❑ pants or pants/skirts/dresses
- ❑ belts
- ❑ dress shirts/blouses
- ❑ sweaters
- ❑ jackets/blazers/ties
- ❑ socks or pantyhose/slips
- ❑ underwear/panties & bras
- ❑ accessories/jewelry
- ❑ shoes
- ❑ _____
- ❑ _____

❑ *Formal wear*
(Consider the number of each formal outfit item that you will need)
- ❑ dress pants/suits/tuxedo
- ❑ dresses/gowns
- ❑ accessories/jewelry
- ❑ socks or pantyhose/slips
- ❑ underwear/panties & bras
- ❑ dress shoes

☐ _____

☐ _____

☐ *Other Clothing items*

    ☐ pajamas

    ☐ lingerie

    ☐ slippers

    ☐ robe

    ☐ _____

    ☐ _____

Miscellaneous items:

☐ An additional set of the important document photocopies as packed in your carry on

☐ Travel tour books, Tourism Bureau Information numbers

☐ Journal

☐ Special honeymoon gift for your new spouse

☐ Any romantic items or favorite accessories

☐ Extra film and camera batteries

☐ Plastic bags for dirty laundry

☐ Large plastic or nylon tote bag for bringing home new purchases

☐ Small sewing kit and safety pins

☐ Travel alarm clock

☐ Travel iron, Lint brush

☐ Compact umbrella, Fold up rain slickers

☐ Hand held tape recorder (for recorded memory journal or for bringing along your favorite, romantic tapes) and/or videocamera

☐ Copy of *Naughty Games for the Honeymoon*, a playful book containing fifty sensual, fun, and exciting games to fill your honeymoon with hot and passionate sex. This book is published by Wedding Solutions Publishing, Inc. and is available at most major bookstores nationwide. Please refer to "Other Great Wedding Products" to order your copy by mail.

☐ _____

For International travel:

❑   Passports/visas

❑   Electric converters and adapter plugs

❑   Copy of appropriate forms showing proof of required vaccinations/inoculations

❑   _____

Other items to bring ...

❑   _____

❑   _____

❑   _____

❑   _____

❑   _____

❑   _____

ITEMS TO LEAVE BEHIND (with a trusted contact person):

❑   Photocopy of all travel details (complete itineraries, names, addresses, and telephone numbers)

❑   Photocopy of credit cards along with 24 hour telephone number to report loss or theft. (Be sure to get the number to call when traveling abroad. It will be a different number than their U.S. 1-800 number.)

❑   Photocopy of travelers checks along with 24 hour telephone number to report loss or theft

❑   Photocopy of passport identification page, along with date and place of issuance

❑   Photocopy of drivers license

❑   Any irreplaceable items

*T*ELL US ABOUT YOUR WEDDING

We would greatly appreciate your writing to us after your honeymoon to let us know how your wedding went and how much the *Easy Wedding Planning Workbook and Organizer* helped you in planning your wedding. We will use this information to continue improving this extensive wedding planner, and we may even use your story in our upcoming book about wedding experiences. We might even ask you to participate in some of our future radio and TV tours where you can tell your own story to the public! Feel free to use additional sheets, if necessary.

Dear Alex & Elizabeth:

I want to tell you that *Easy Wedding Planning Workbook and Organizer*: (helped a lot), (helped a little), in planning my wedding. I especially liked your section on _____
_____. My wedding was on _____ and it was: (a complete success), (a wild party), (a boring event), (a complete disaster), (the most stressful day of my life).

My comments about your book are: _____
_____
_____
_____
_____

I wish your book had given me information about: _____
_____
_____
_____
_____

The best thing about my wedding was: _____
_____
_____
_____
_____
_____

The worst thing about my wedding was: _____
_____
_____
_____
_____
_____

The funniest thing about my wedding was: _____

_____

_____

_____

_____

_____

What made my wedding special or unique was: _____

_____

_____

_____

_____

_____

My wedding would have been much better if: _____

_____

_____

_____

_____

_____

This is to authorize Wedding Solutions Publishing, Inc. to use our story in any of their upcoming books. Wedding Solutions Publishing, Inc. (can), (cannot) use our name when telling our story. I also (am), (am not) interested in participating in a radio/TV interview tour.

Bride's Name _____   Bride's Signature _____

Groom's Name _____   Groom's Signature _____

Address _____

Home Number _____   Work Number _____

Fold in three and mail to Wedding Solutions Publishing, Inc.

Place
Stamp
Here

Wedding Solutions Publishing, Inc.
6347 Caminito Tenedor
San Diego, CA 92120

YOUR BRIDAL SUPERSTORE

The Ultimate Online Wedding Source℠

www.YourBridalSuperstore.com

Proudly Presents
The largest selection of wedding products...offering thousands
of accessories, invitations, jewelry, gifts, and much more

www.YourBridalSuperstore.com offers unparalleled customer
service, highest quality products, lowest price guarantee, and
free shipping*. Find everything you need for the wedding of
your dreams in one convenient location.

This catalog contains a small sample of the thousands of products available at:

www.YourBridalSuperstore.com

*Log onto *www.YourBridalSuperstore.com* for details.

A Pearl Heart Candle.
#37300   ~ $32.95
Pearl Heart Tapers.
#37310   ~ $32.95

B Silver-Finish Unity
Candle Holder. 12½" long.
#23800   ~ $27.95

C Western Candle.
#37700   ~ $32.95
Western Tapers.
#37710   ~ $32.95

D Brass-Finish Unity
Candle Holder. 12½" long.
#23700   ~ $27.95

E Iridescent Pearl Candle.
#37400   ~ $32.95
Iridescent Pearl Tapers.
#37410   ~ $32.95

▼ **E, F**

A, B ▶

*Hand-carved candles add a
beautiful touch to the wedding cerem
Single 9" candle or pair of 11¾" tap*

C, D ▶

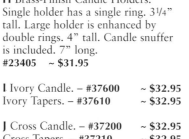

G, H ▶

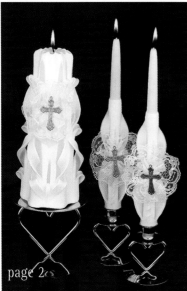

F Heart Candle Holder Set.
#38100   ~ $31.95

G Unity Candles. Available in white
only. Set of 3 candles. 8" tall.
#20901   ~ $26.95

H Brass-Finish Candle Holders.
Single holder has a single ring. 3¼"
tall. Large holder is enhanced by
double rings. 4" tall. Candle snuffer
is included. 7" long.
#23405   ~ $31.95

I Ivory Candle. – #37600   ~ $32.95
Ivory Tapers. – #37610   ~ $32.95

J Cross Candle. – #37200   ~ $32.95
Cross Tapers. – #37210   ~ $32.95

◀ J

I ▶

Rich, Lacy Presentations

◄ A, B

Organza ribbon-striped trim is the crisp flourish making this set stand out as innovative and fresh.

A Garter – **#79901**   ~ **$7.95**

B Heart Pillow. 10" x 10".
#79801   ~ **$23.95**

C ►

C Square ivory pillow with iridescent pearl trim has a tailored look with classical appeal. 13" x 13".
#82403   ~ **$24.95**

D Square Pillow. 13" x 13".
#80401   ~ **$22.95**

E Garter – **#80501**   ~ **$7.50**

◄ D, E

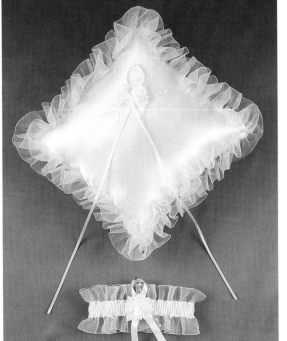

▼ F

F Romantic white treasure chest ring holder has lacy, pearlized edgings. 4" x 4¹/₂" x 3".
#20800   ~ **$24.95**

G Opulent ivory ring-bearer treasure chest is encrusted with decorative faux jewel detailing. Provides magnificent presentation of the cherished ring. Measures 4" x 4¹/₂" x 3".
#20803   ~ **$24.95**

G ►

A Bouquet of Lovely Frills and Flourishes

◄ B, C

A ►

A Contemporary garter of organza artistry has a lovely decorative pearl detail. – #27801 ~ **$17.50**

B Ribbon-striped garter exudes fun and flare as well as beauty. – #79901 ~ **$7.95**

C Wide 2" eyelet lace makes a garter to complement springtime innocence. – #86301 ~ **$16.95**

D Charming chiffon garter features strings of pearls and a dainty blue flower. – #72201 ~ **$8.95**

E Filigree, scalloped-edge heart motif lace garter. #84501 ~ **$17.95**

F "One to Keep and One to Throw" Garter Set. Our most popular deluxe garter for the bride to keep and a less expensive garter for the traditional throw. White Set – #85901 ~ **$13.95**   Blue Set – #85907 ~ **$13.95**

G Dangling Pearls Garter (shown on model's leg). Laceless simplicity with elegant pearl highlights. #27501 ~ **$11.95**

H A garter with the popular iridescent look. The detail of triple flower buds add appeal. #80501 ~ **$7.50**

I A delicate garter featuring frothy puffs of chiffon. – #87101 ~ **$9.50**

◄ D

◄ E

F ▼

G ►

◄ G

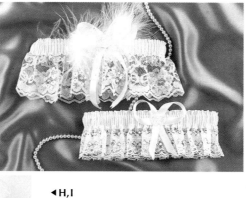

◄ H, I

Enhancements for the Wedding Cake

Personalize your wedding cake with mix & match cake tops and figurines. Items are sold separately.

▼ A

◄ B

A Bride and Groom. Ivory with gold accents. 7 1/4" tall. #32203 ~ $29.95

B Bride and Groom. 8 1/2" tall. #13301 ~ $29.95

▼ C, D, E, F

Black Groom. 5" tall. – #12302   ~ $6.70

Black Bride. 5" tall. – #12202   ~ $6.70

White Groom. 5" tall. – #12301   ~ $6.70

White Bride. 5" tall. – #12201   ~ $6.70

variations may occur in the hair and tuxedo colors.

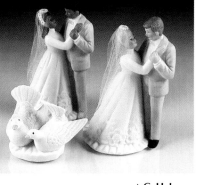

▲ G, H, I

G Black Bride and Groom. 5 1/4" tall. – #29932 ~ $14.95

H White Bride and Groom. 5 1/4" tall. – #29931 ~ $14.95

I Porcelain Doves. 3 1/2" tall. #14163 ~ $6.70

▲ J

J Bears in a Swing tops a cake with delightful fun. A great momento for remembering the celebration. 5" tall. #13200 ~ $10.95

◄ K

▼ L, M

K Choose from frilly white or ivory versions of cake top with versatile mirror platform and blown glass arch. Full height is 8 3/4", base is 2 1/2" tall, circle diameter 4".
White – #17301   ~ $47.95
Ivory – #17303   ~ $47.95

L Pig Bride and Groom. 3 1/2" tall. – #12400 ~ $9.95

M Cow Bride and Groom. 3 1/2" tall. – #12450 ~ $9.95

page 5

Pillows
Candles
Knife
Glasses
Garter
Basket

GLIMMERING SATIN COLLECTION
White satin & the impeccable pearl.

16901 ~ $37.95
White Ring Pillow – White satin 8" square pillow with white chiffon bow and faux pearl

14401 ~ $17.95
Garter – White satin and chiffon bow with faux pearl

12101 ~ $53.95
White Flower Girl Basket – 8" tall with white chiffon trim (flowers not included)

17901 ~ $27.95
Bridal Purse – White satin 5" x 9" clutch purse trimmed with pearl accents and faux pearl

33001 ~ $35.95
Unity Candle – 9" white candle with satin and chiffon bow and faux pearl

33101 ~ $27.95
Set of Tapers – 12" white tapers with satin and chiffon bows with faux pearl

32326 ~ $73.95
Silver Beaded Serving Set – Features white satin and chiffon bows with faux pearls, 10" server, 12" knife

33792 ~ $109.95
Crystal Flute Set – Elegant flutes with frosted glass and accented with white satin and chiffon bows with faux pearl stand 10¾" tall and hold 6½ ounces ea

14201 ~ $17.95
Accent Bow Set – White satin and chiffon bows with faux pearls

All above items are also available in:

Ecru

TOASTING GLASSES

HEART-SHAPED GOBLET ▶

A toast from the heart.

20660 ~ $57.95
The unique two-piece silver-plated wedding goblet
stands 5¾" tall and each piece holds 5 ounces

◀ SILVER AND GOLD FLUTES

Gleaming silver, glimmering gold

20500 ~ $59.95
Silver-plated flutes featuring stems with gold
band accents are 9" tall and hold 7 ounces

SILVER-PLATED FLUTES ▶

Silver elegance.

20350 ~ $49.95
Traditional long-stemmed flutes
stand 9½" tall and hold 7¼ ounces

All toasting glasses can be personalized for an additional charge.

SERVING SETS

GOLD SERVING SET ▲
Scintillating gold.

32518 ~ $39.95
Gold-plated handles with stainless steel blades,
10" server, 12" knife

CRYSTAL-HANDLED SERVING SET ▲
Peerless in craft.

32400 ~ $63.95
Crystal-handled serving set with stainless steel blades,
10" server, 12" knife

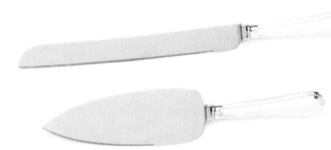

SILVER BEADED SERVING SET ▲
Lustrous silver.

32325 ~ $59.95
Elegant silver-plated handles are edged in fine
beading, 10" server, 12" knife

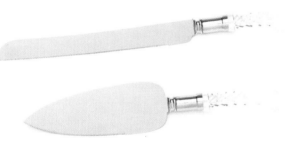

CRYSTAL SERVING SET ▲
Crystal at its best.

32500 ~ $91.95
Handles are made of 24% lead crystal,
10½" server, 12½" knife

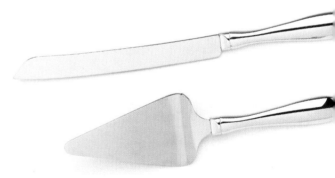

SILVER-PLATED SERVING SET ▲
Simply silver.

32825 ~ $99.95
Silver-plated with handsomely sculpted handles,
11" server, 13½" knife

◄ SILVER & GOLD SERVING SET
Silver & a touch of gold.

32600 ~ $37.95
Elegant silver-plated handles feature gold
accents, 10½" server, 12½" knife

All Serving Sets can be personalized for an additional charge.

FAVOURS
CAKE BOXES
CANDY WRAP

72302   72300   72301   72306

HEART-SHAPED FAVOUR BOXES

72302   ~ $5.95
White 3½" x 4" favour boxes are prepunched with heart-shaped holes for threading the included 7" precut white chiffon ribbon (12 per package)

BOW FAVOUR BOXES

72300   ~ $3.95
White 2¾" x 1½" x 2" favour boxes with bow-shaped closures (12 per package)

HEART-HANDLED FAVOUR BOXES

72301   ~ $3.95
White 3½" x 2¼" x 1¼" favour boxes with heart-shaped handles (contents not included) (12 per package)

TREASURE CHEST FAVOUR BOXES

72306   ~ $5.95
White 2¾" x 2⅛" x 1¾" treasure chest-shaped boxes with moiré finish (contents not included) (12 per package)

FLORAL CAKE BOXES

72305   ~ $5.95
White 3½" x 3½" x 3" boxes with pastel floral pattern (contents not included) (12 per package)

SILVER & GOLD GLITTER FAVOUR BAGS

72325 (Silver)   ~ $31.95

72318 (Gold)   ~ $31.95
The 4" x 5" favour bags feature white netting with silver glitter swirls or ecru netting with gold glitter. Ribbon is attached for tying closed (contents not included)   (12 per package)

WHITE & ECRU CONE FAVOUR BOXES

72501 (White) ~ $17.95

72503 (Ecru) ~ $17.95
White or ecru 6¼" cone boxes with filigree pattern and flower-shaped handle. 12" matching chiffon ribbon included (12 per package)

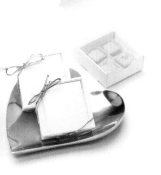

SILVER & GOLD FOIL FAVOUR BOXES

72304 (Silver) ~ $7.95

72303 (Gold)   ~ $7.95
White Favour boxes with silver or gold foil border, 2½" x 2½" x 1", and pretied silver or gold cords (contents not included) (12 per package)

GOLD & SILVER CANDY BAR WRAPPERS

64718 (Gold) ~ $7.95
64725 (Silver) ~ $7.95
The 5¼" x 5½" wrappers are preprinted with verse as shown in black ink. (chocolate bars not included) (12 per package)

SHEER WRAP FAVOUR BOXES

72307   ~ $9.95
White 2¼" x 1¾" x 2" favour boxes wrapped in translucent overlay with filigree pattern and white chiffon ribbon. Overlay is prepunched with holes for inserting the ribbon (12 per package)

SHEER HEART FAVOUR ENVELOPES

72308   ~ $5.95
Translucent white paper with pearlescent design. Envelope has heart-shaped closures and folds to 2⅞" square (contents not included) (12 per package)

WHITE CANDY BAR WRAPPERS

64701   ~ $7.95
The 5¼" x 5½" wrappers are preprinted with "Thank You" verse as shown in black ink. (chocolate bars not included) (12 per package)

BRIDESMAID & MAID OF HONOR ▲ CARDS

61000 (Bridesmaid) ~ $5.95

61100 (Maid of Honor) ~ $2.50
Appreciation cards feature a floral border and verse as shown. Bridesmaid cards are sold in packs of three; maid of honor cards are sold individually. Envelopes are included

SILVER PHOTO ▲ FRAME ALBUM

60700 ~ $27.95
A silver frame forms the cover of an album that holds 100 4" x 6" photographs (ideal for engraving)

BRIDESMAID ▲ PHOTO MAT

60900 ~ $9.95
Ecru 10" x 8" mat printed in taupe ink with "Bridesmaid / Best of Friends"

BRIDESMAID CANDLE ▶

60500 ~ $15.95
Clear glass box holds a vanilla-scented candle. The lid features "To my Bridesmaid...and special friend" preprinted in gold.

◀ PICTURE FRAMES

63100 ~ $5.95
Solid brass picture frame measures 2" x 3"

63000 ~ $5.95
Silver-plated picture frame measures 2" x 3"

◀ HEART COMPACT

61600 ~ $15.95
Heart-shaped silver- and gold-plated mirror compact (ideal for engraving)

◀ CHERRY WOOD AND PEWTER BOX

58900 ~ $57.95
Wooden box is 7¼" x 5½" x 2". A pewter plaque is accented with flowers and "Friendship Comes From The Heart." (ideal for engraving)

SILVER ROSE ▶ KEEPSAKE BOX

61500 ~ $13.95
Silver-tone 3" x 3" x 1½" box is decorated with a sculpted rose (ideal for engraving)

◀ COMPACT CALCULATOR

62800 ~ $29.95
3½" x 2" silver-plated calculator features embossed stripes and oval with solar-powered calculator inside (cover of calculator ideal for engraving)

BRIDESMAID BOOKMARKS

62600 ~ $19.95
Bookmarks are accented with pastel flowers, "With Love & Thanks" and verse shown printed in gold ink and 7" precut white chiffon ribbon (package of six)

◀ MAKEUP BRUSHES

62900 ~ $41.95
Six-piece silver-plated cosmetic brush set with black satin carrying pouch

-D) Pearl-embossed flowers form a heart on the covers of these albums, ...nding romance to your wedding memories. Choose white or ecru cov-...rs to match your wedding. Personalize the albums with your names and ...edding date engraved on a gold-tone plate to match the gold titles. **...lease specify names and wedding date to be engraved.**

,B) The bookbound album measures 9" x 11" and contains 52 pages, ...cluding space to record 240 guests and 224 gifts.

...) **WF8W52B** *White Pearl Heart Album*..................................$38.50
   WF8W52P *Personalized*..................$5.00 Engraving fee + $38.50
...) **WF10003B** *Ecru Pearl Heart Album* $38.50
   WF10003P *Personalized*..................$5.00 Engraving fee + $38.50

,D) The matching guest book measures 7¾" x 5¾" and contains ...pace to hold the signatures of 600 guests.

...) **WFW52B** *White Pearl Heart Guest Book* $20.50
   WFW52P *Personalized*.....................$5.00 Engraving fee + $20.50
...) **WF10006B** *Ecru Pearl Heart Guest Book*...........................$20.50
   WF10006P *Personalized*..................$5.00 Engraving fee + $20.50

...) White raw silk and a beaded, white satin floral appliqué create a look ...f fresh beauty on this guest book. Inside are pages to hold the signa-...ures of up to 650 guests. The 9" x 7" book may be personalized with ...our names and wedding date engraved on a gold-tone plate. **Please ...pecify names and wedding date.** A matching pen is sold below.

...**F3900B** *Floral Appliqué Guest Book* $70.95
...**F3900P** *Personalized*.........................$5.00 Engraving fee + $70.95

...) An oval pen base is covered in white raw silk, trimmed with satin cord ...nd adorned with a beaded, white satin floral appliqué. The base measures ..." x 4" and features a swivel holder for the 6" gold-tone pen included.

...**F0220** *Floral Appliqué Pen* $38.50

...) Make registering your guests an elegant experience with this beau-...ful guest book. Covered in white moiré satin, it is adorned with a ...laque of richly sculpted white porcelain on the front and may be per-...onalized with your names and wedding date engraved on a gold-tone ...late inside. Gold-accented pages hold the signatures of nearly 900 ...uests. The guest book is 8" x 5½" and ties securely closed with white ...atin ribbon. **Please specify names and wedding date to be engraved.** ...Matching pen is sold below.

...**F10004B** *Porcelain Guest Book* $51.50
...**F10004P** *Personalized*.........................$5.00 Engraving fee + $51.50

...) A heart-shaped white porcelain base is covered in embossed scrolls ...nd filigree. A gold-tone pen rests securely in a swivel holder attached ...o the 3½" x 3½" base; the pen and base together measure 8" tall. The ...en set makes a lovely complement to the porcelain-accented guest ...ook sold above.

...**F10007** *Gold Pen with Porcelain Base* $34.95

CT920

GB454
GB455

GB452

G920

PEN920

K925

CT920 9.5" Gazebo Caketop $40.95

GB452 10.5" Guest Book W/Pen **White, Ivory** $33.45

GB454 10" Heart Book **White, Ivory** $50.95

GB455 10" Heart Book W/Pen **White, Ivory** $52.95

G920 8.5" Toasting Glasses $33.45

PEN920 3.5" Pen Set **Painted** $20.45

K925 12" Knife & Server Set **Painted** $24.45

* All items this page available in white and painted only, unless oth...
specified.

BX920

BX920 5" Trinket Box **White, Painted**
$23.95

KS510
Set of 6

LG481

KS510 Set of 6 Cake Charms **Silver** $35.45

LG481 Daisy Garter **White** $8.45

GB120 8.5" Guest Book $24.95

SP100 8.5" Easel $8.45

SP160 8" x 10" Frame $23.95

SP150 5" x 7" Frame $11.95

SP140 3.5" x 5" Frame $8.45

SP110 6" Pen Set $11.45

FR982 4" x 6" Photo Stand $10.95

PH980 4" x 6" Photo Album $23.95

FR981 3.5" x 5" Photo Stand $9.45

FR980 3" x 5" Frame $12.00

* All items on this page as shown.

RP800

LG802

LG285

RP110

LG804

KS100 BI

KS100 SP

LG286

LG185

LG801

KS100 HT

LG280

RP800 11" Ring Pillow **White, Ivory** $22.95

RP110 8" Ring Pillow **White, Ivory** $21.45

LG185 Something Blue Garter **White, Ivory, Blue** $9.45

LG280 Keepsake Garter **White, Ivory** $18.00

LG285 Keepsake Garter **White, Ivory** $16.95

LG286 Keepsake Garter **White, Ivory** $11.95

LG801 Tossing Garter **White, Ivory, Blue** $8.45

LG802 Garter Set **White, Ivory** $18.00

LG804 Garter W/Pence **White, Ivory** $15.95

KS100 BI 1.5" Bible $8.45

KS100 HT 1" Blue Heart $6.00

KS100 SP Six Pence $6.00

ORDER ONLINE AT:
YourBridalSuperstore.com

ELEGANT PENS...
for a beautiful guest registry

A) Covered in white satin and accented with a satin bow, braided trim and faux pearl, this pen base will accent your guest book beautifully. A white holder supports a pen with a 12" white ostrich plume. The oval base me $3\frac{3}{4}$" x $5\frac{1}{2}$".
WF1150 Satin Bow and Pearl Base with Plume Pen...............................$

B) A heart-shaped white porcelain base is covered in embossed scrolls a gree. A gold-tone pen rests securely in a swivel holder attached to the $3\frac{1}{2}$" base; the pen and base together measure 8" tall. The pen set makes a lovel plement to the porcelain-accented guest book sold on page 11.
WF10007 Porcelain Heart Base Pen ....$

C) A gold-tone pen in a heart-shaped crystal base is a lovely accessory fc guest book and a perfect keepsake after the wedding. It also makes specia for attendants and friends. Pen and base measure 8" tall; base is $3\frac{1}{4}$" acros
WF188G Gold Pen with Crystal Heart Base ....$

D) Accent your Western wedding with this 3" x $2\frac{1}{2}$" pen base covered in satin and trimmed with satin cord, ribbon, hearts and a gold-tone Weste charm. A white pen with gold accents rests in the gold swivel holder. The ba pen stand $8\frac{1}{2}$" tall.
WF28 Western Base Pen..$

E) Faceted lead crystal forms a guest book pen base of exquisite quali sparkle — your guest book table will certainly be eye-catching! The $3\frac{1}{4}$" ter base features a silver-tone swivel stand to hold a silver-tone pen. Togeth base and pen measure 8" tall.
WF1317 Silver Pen with Round Crystal Base ....$

F) Genuine pewter is sculpted with hearts and flowers for a uniquely ro guest book pen. The $2\frac{1}{4}$" diameter base features a foam-lined bottom to pro surface of your guest book table. A $6\frac{3}{4}$" pen sculpted with the same pretty rests in the swivel holder attached to the base. Together, the base and pe $8\frac{3}{4}$" tall.
WF807 Pewter Pen and Base ....$

G) Plume pens add tradition to your guest book. Gold-tone filigree base pens with 14" ostrich plumes, which are available in emerald, burgundy, mauve, pink, white, peach, red, royal blue, teal, ecru, black and hot pink write in blue ink. **Specify plume color choice.**
WFAPC25 Plume Pen ....$

H) A white or ecru pen with a 14" matching ostrich plume rests in a contem Lucite base. The base is available personalized with a gold-tone plate engrave your names and wedding date. **Specify color, names and wedding date.**
WFPC27B Lucite Base Pen..$
WFPC27P Personalized.....................................$5.00 Engraving fee + $

I) Silver plating makes this sleek and elegant pen set shimmer. The heav base measures $2\frac{3}{4}$" x 3" x $1\frac{1}{4}$" and features a felt-covered bottom to prote table. The base and pen together stand $5\frac{1}{2}$" tall.
WF3201 Silver-Plated Base and Pen ....$

www.YourBridalSuperstore.com

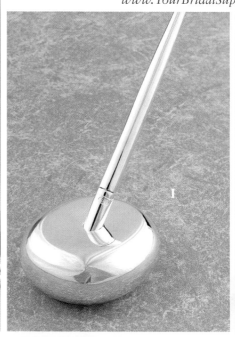

page 16

PEARL-EMBOSSED NAPKINS

A-E) Make your good taste evident at each place setting with pearl-embossed napkins. Your names and wedding date are printed in the lettering style shown. Choose an ink or foil color listed below. Napkins are available only with the pearl designs shown; ink or foil color applies to personalization. Available in luncheon (13" x 13") and beverage (9 1/2" x 9 1/2") sizes. **Please specify names, date and ink or foil color.**

A) White napkins feature a pearl-embossed bouquet; your names and wedding date are printed beneath the design. See pricing at right. Please specify names, date and ink or foil color. Ink and foil colors listed below.

WF188B White Pearl Bouquet Beverage
WF188L White Pearl Bouquet Luncheon

A-E			
Pearl Beverage Napkins	50	42.00
Pearl Beverage Napkins	add'l 50	18.00
Pearl Luncheon Napkins	50	42.00
Pearl Luncheon Napkins	add'l 50	18.00

B,C) A pearl-embossed floral heart adorns ecru or white napkins. Your names and date are printed within the heart design. Please note: Beverage napkins feature your names and wedding date printed in the elegant block lettering shown. See pricing above. Please specify names, date and ink or foil color. Ink and foil colors listed at right.

B) WF197B Ecru Pearl Floral Heart Beverage
   WF197L Ecru Pearl Floral Heart Luncheon
C) WF194B White Pearl Floral Heart Beverage
   WF194L White Pearl Floral Heart Luncheon

INK COLORS

Black, brown, fuchsia, hunter, lilac, navy, periwinkle, pink, plum, purple, red, rosewood, sage, taupe, teal, wine

FOIL COLORS

Blue, gold, hunter, pink, purple, red, silver, teal, white

Please note: For best results, choose gold or silver foil for black, navy, purple, teal and wine napkins.

D) White napkins are embossed with fresh and fun daisies in pearl. Your names and wedding date are printed beneath the design. See pricing above. Please specify names, date and ink or foil color. Ink and foil colors listed above.

WF161B White Pearl Daisy Beverage
WF161L White Pearl Daisy Luncheon

E) A pearl couple design adds romance to these white napkins. Your names and wedding date are printed beneath the design. See pricing above. Please specify names, date and ink or foil color. Ink and foil colors listed above.

WF290B White Pearl Couple Beverage
WF290L White Pearl Couple Luncheon

F

Sweetheart Beverage Napkins	50	46.50
Sweetheart Beverage Napkins	add'l 50	22.50
Sweetheart Luncheon Napkins	50	46.50
Sweetheart Luncheon Napkins	add'l 50	22.50

F) A sweet image of young love is printed in black and white on white napkins. A single red rose adds color. Your names and date are printed beneath the design. Choose an ink or foil color listed above for personalization. Available in luncheon (13" x 13") and beverage (9 1/2" x 9 1/2") sizes. Please specify names, date and ink or foil color. Please specify names, date and ink or foil color. Ink and foil colors listed above.

WF215B White Sweetheart Beverage
WF215L White Sweetheart Luncheon

G

	50	100	add'l 25
Thank you - Printed	53.90	57.90	12.30
Thank you - Blank	19.50		9.00

H-J

	50	100	add'l 25
Thank you - Printed	53.90	57.90	12.50
Thank you - Blank	19.50		9.00

K-L

	50	100	add'l 25
Thank you - Printed	62.90	66.90	14.25
Thank you - Blank	21.00		10.00

POPULAR THANK YOU VERSES

These verses may be used on the inside of your thank you cards. You may choose from those shown below or write your own.

TY5

With sincere appreciation,
we both send thanks to you
for your very lovely gift
and for your thoughtful wishes, too.

Bethany and Roger Zimmerman

TY6

A loving note can barely say
all we felt that magic day.
A heartfelt thanks is sent to you
for your thoughtful gift and wishes, too.

Maria and Jerry Steinback

TY8

Words cannot express
the joy that we feel
remembering that you shared
the beginning of our new life together.
Thank you for your very thoughtful gift.

Mr. and Mrs. Russell Jackson

TY38

Being remembered
In such a nice way
Means a lot more than
Just "thank you" can say!
Mr. and Mrs. Kenneth Isder

G) Silver hearts add sparkle to this white thank you note.
WF0015 Hearts

H) Young love is captured in this black-and-white portrait on white paper accented by a gold foil verse and a red rose
WF7995 Young Love

I) Rich burgundy roses and green leaves are embossed in pearl on these ecru notes. "Thank You" glistens in gold foil.
WF1085 Burgundy Roses

J) An ornate pearl-embossed border frames a gold foil "Thank You" on this bright white note.
WF1245 Pearl Embossed

K) Translucent white paper* is embossed with a swirling filigree pattern and features a gold foil "Thank You."
WF1395 Translucent Embossed Swirls

L) Beautiful pastel flowers are printed on sheer white paper*, and "Thank You" sparkles in gold foil.
WF6425 Translucent Floral

* Because of the unique, translucent quality of the paper, please allow for some natural color variation. Be sure to use permanent ink when writing on these notes to prevent smearing.

A,B) A double band of shimmering pearl highlights the em border of these elegant bright white thank you notes. "Tha gleams in your choice of gold or silver foil.
A) WF1525 Gold/Pearl Panel
B) WF1535 Silver/Pearl Panel

	50	100	add'l 25
Thank you - Printed	53.90	57.90	12.30
Thank you - Blank	19.50		9.00

C-J) These traditional thank you notes could not be more l For added elegance, an embossed rose adorns notes H-J.
C) WF8655 White/rainbow foil
D) WF1235 White/purple foil
E) WF9995 White/hunter foil
F) WF5015 White/navy foil
G) WF7075 Ecru/gold foil
H) WF1475 White/black foil/rose
I) WF1145 White/gold foil/rose
J) WF0465 Ivory/gold foil/rose

	50	100	add'l 25
Thank you - Printed	43.90	47.90	10.20
Thank you - Blank	15.50		7.00

L) Pretty pastel flowers and titles in gold foil make these w notes a lovely way to express your thanks to your weddin party and others. The set includes 29 blank cards and 30 b envelopes: one card titled "To my Best Man," one "To my of Honor," one "To my Matron of Honor," one "To my Per Attendant," one "To my Flowergirl," one "To my Ringbear five cards with "To my Bridesmaid," five cards with "To m Groomsman," four cards with "To my Usher," and nine car with "Thank You for Your Services."
WF3805

Thank you - Wedding Party	set	8.95

K) Gold and silver rings are perfect for securing your scrolls, decorating favors, using as napkin rings...and more! Sold in packages of 144.
WFP92G Gold Rings
WFP92S Silver Rings

Gold Rings - WFP92G	7.90
Silver Rings - WFP92S	7.90

PLACE CARDS
seating your guests in style

A-J) Personalized place cards direct your guests to their places at the table with beautiful designs that reflect your wedding theme. Prices include printing in black ink with your first names, wedding date and lines to write guests' names and table number. For printing in a colorful ink, add $7.00. **Please specify names, wedding date and ink color.**

A) Add a unique touch to each place setting with these personalized heart-shaped place cards designed to attach to the stems of your toasting flutes. Each 3 3/4" X 2 3/4" white card features a pearl heart outline and rose design. A slot and opening at the top makes it easy for you to secure the cards around the stems of your flutes.
WF1808 Flute Stem Place Cards

A

Place card - WF1808	50	40.90
Place card - WF1808	add'l 25	17.50

B) Sheer white paper with a subtle pinstripe design creates these clearly elegant place cards. An embossed scroll frame surrounds your personalization on the front. Place cards measure 41/4" x 2 1/8" Because of the translucent quality of the paper, please allow for some natural color variation. When writing on translucent place cards, be sure to use permanent ink to prevent smearing. Design only as shown.
WF6428 Translucent Place Cards

C,D) Forever Floral paper is an elegant backdrop for place cards. Place cards measure 4 1/4" x 2 1/8"
C) WF9008 White
D) WF8008 Ecru

E,F) An ornate border is embossed around the edges of these white or ecru place cards. Place cards measure 4 3/8" x 2 1/8" Design only as shown.
E) WF2248 White Embossed
F) WF3018 Ecru Embossed

G,H) Three embossed panels surround large bright white or ecru place cards with elegance. Place cards measure 4 3/8" x 2 1/4". Design only as shown.
G) WF91 White
H) WF976PC Ecru

I,J) Crisp ecru, white or bright white (not shown) place cards let you create the look! Place cards measure 4 3/8" x 2 1/8"
I) WF0328 White Vellum
J) WF2388 Ecru Vellum
  WF9108 Bright White Vellum.

B

Place card - WF6428	50	47.90
Place card - WF6428	add'l 25	11.50

C-D

Place card - WF9008	50	47.90
Place card - WF9008	add'l 25	11.50
Place card - WF8008	50	47.90
Place card - WF8008	add'l 25	11.50

E-F

Place card - WF2248	50	47.90
Place card - WF2248	add'l 25	11.50
Place card - WF3018	50	47.90
Place card - WF3018	add'l 25	11.50

G-H

Place card - WF91	50	47.90
Place card - WF91	add'l 25	11.50
Place card - WF976PC	50	47.90
Place card - WF976PC	add'l 25	11.50

I-J

Place card - WF0328	50	44.90
Place card - WF0328	add'l 25	10.50
Place card - WF2388	50	44.90
Place card - WF2388	add'l 25	10.50
Place card - WF9108	50	44.90
Place card - WF9108	add'l 25	10.50

For ink and design options, log onto www.YourBridalSuperstore.com

FAVOR BOOKMARKS AND SCROLLS
meaningful, memorable keepsakes

BOOKMARKS
Printed with your names, wedding date and choice of verse, bookmarks are an elegant, personal way to thank your guests! Select a verse from those shown on the bookmarks, or write your own verse for an additional $25.00 charge. Please be sure to specify the verse when ordering. Pricing is for black ink. Your verse, names, design and wedding date may be printed on the 2 1/4" x 8 1/4" bookmarks in a colorful ink for an additional $7.00 charge. The following colored inks are available: brown, fuchsia, gold, grey, hunter, lilac, navy, periwinkle, pink, plum, purple, red, rosewood, sage, silver, taupe, teal and wine. Verses available only in the lettering style shown on the bookmarks. Satin tassels are free with your bookmarks. Please specify the tassel color when ordering. Choose from silver, teal, white, emerald, black, ecru, gold, purple or pink tassels or hunter. If a tassel color is not noted, tassels that match the paper color will be sent. Tassels are not attached.

Please specify your names, wedding date, verse, design, ink color and tassel color.

A-C

Bookmark - WF605BKMK	50	47.90
Bookmark - WF605BKMK	add'l 25	18.50
Bookmark - WF603BKMK	50	45.90
Bookmark - WF603BKMK	add'l 25	18.00
Bookmark - WF30122BKMK	50	43.90
Bookmark - WF30122BKMK	add'l 50	35.00

A-C) Translucent white bookmarks are available with a floral pattern, an embossed filigree pattern or smooth your wedding style. **Because of the translucent quality paper, please allow for some natural color variation.**
A) WF605BKMK Floral Translucent, shown with verse
B) WF603BKMK Embossed Filigree Translucent, shown verse FB106 and design 1035C
C) WF30122BKMK Smooth Translucent, shown with ve and design 1104C

SCROLLS
Scrolls are a popular way to thank guests for making your day special. Each 5" x 7" scroll will also be personalized with your names and wedding date. Prices shown are for printing in black ink; for printing in a colored ink, add $7.00. Scrolls may be rolled and secured with scroll rings (item K sold on page 19) and handed to guests before the ceremony or placed at each plate at the reception. **Please indicate names, wedding date, design (items D-G), lettering style, verse and ink color.**

D,E) Scrolls made from Forever Floral paper let you thank guests with style.
Choose creamy ecru or bright white paper.
D) WF8006 Ecru Forever Floral, shown with verse SC107 and design 2637C
E) WF9006 White Forever Floral, shown with verse SC113 and design 1930C

Scroll - WF8006	100	
Scroll - WF8006	add'l	
Scroll - WF9006	100	
Scroll - WF9006	add'l	

F,G) Rich, smooth vellum papers give these scrolls traditional appeal.
F) WF1466 Ecru Vellum (no deckle edge), shown with verse SC107 and design 1064C
G) WF2026 White Vellum Deckle, shown with verse SC102 and design 1464C

Scroll - WF1466	100	40.90
Scroll - WF1466	add'l 50	18.50
Scroll - WF2026	100	40.90
Scroll - WF2026	add'l 50	18.50

H,I) Scrolls of sheer white paper are printed with an all-over filigree pattern in glossy ink or with a colorful floral pattern for unique elegance. **Because of the translucent quality of the paper, please allow for some natural variation in color.**
H) WF9426 Filigree Translucent
I) WF6426 Floral Translucent

Scroll - WF9426	100	47.90
Scroll - WF9426	add'l 50	20.50
Scroll - WF6426	100	47.90
Scroll - WF6426	add'l 50	20.50

WEDDING PROGRAMS
elegant guides to your ceremony

A-E) Wedding programs welcome guests to your ceremony and provide important information. Prices are for 70 lines of copy in black ink; for a colorful ink add $7.00. A message up to 14 lines long may be printed on the back for $25.00 extra. Choose a lettering style for your introductory wording; the remaining copy is printed in block lettering. If you would like a proof copy of your programs, there will be a $25.00 charge. Please allow 48 hours for processing of your proof copy once received, plus shipping time. This also applies to your program order. Because of the amount of wording, we cannot accept phone orders for programs. For complete ordering information, log onto:
www.YourBridalSuperstore.com

A) Pearl-embossed hearts, roses and ribbons gleam on this soft white Z-fold program, and "Our Wedding Service" sparkles in gold foil. Your first names are printed within the hearts in the same lettering style and ink color as your introductory inside wording. **Please specify names.** Folded size: 3 3/4" x 8 1/2"

	50	75	100	add'l 25
Program - WFP1050	92.90	95.90	98.90	21.90

B) A beautiful bouquet of white flowers is captured on this soft white program. "Love One Another" is printed in black beside the floral design. Your program wording is printed inside. Coordinate with any invitation. Folded size: 5 1/2" x 8 1/2"

	50	75	100	add'l 25
Program - WFP657P Printed	77.90	80.90	83.90	18.90
Program - WFP657B Blank			40.90	9.00

C) A black-and-white photograph of charming young sweethearts is enhanced by touches of color to create adorable programs. "This Day I'll Marry My Friend..." appears in white on the front; your program wording is printed inside. Folded size: 5 1/2" x 8 1/2"

	50	75	100	add'l 25
Program - WFP0112P Printed	77.90	80.90	83.90	18.90
Program - WFP0112B Blank			40.90	9.00

TRADITIONAL WHITE ▶

This traditional single panel is featured on a soft white vellum folder. This ensemble features an informal folder. Respond and reception will be a card. 5 1/8" x 7 3/4"
WA203-71

LINER CHOICES:

Plum, Navy, Hunter, Wine, Black, Purple, Rosewood, Silver, Taupe, Pearl, Gold, Sage, Lilac, Peach, Periwinkle, Pink, Red, Sky, Teal

ITEM	ITEM NUMBER	25	50	75
Invitation	WA203-71	51.90	56.90	61.90
Invitation Envelope Flaps	PRTENV	22.00	23.00	26.70
Invitation Liner Envelopes	LINEDENV	4.90	9.80	14.70
Reception Cards	WARW22	31.70	34.10	36.50
Respond Cards	WAEW22-01	39.60	42.70	45.80
Note	WAI406-01	31.70	34.10	36.50
Note Envelope Flaps	PRTENV	22.00	23.00	26.70
Thank You Folder – Blank Inside	WAU406-01	31.70	34.10	36.50

ITEM (cont.)	100	125	150	Add'l 25
Invitation	66.90	81.30	95.70	14.40
Invitation Envelope Flaps	30.40	34.10	37.80	3.70
Invitation Liner Envelopes	19.60	24.50	29.40	4.90
Reception Cards	38.90	47.20	55.50	8.30
Respond Cards	48.90	59.30	69.70	10.40
Note	38.90	47.20	55.50	8.30
Note Envelope Flaps	30.40	34.10	37.80	3.70
Thank You Folder – Blank Inside	38.90	47.20	55.50	8.30

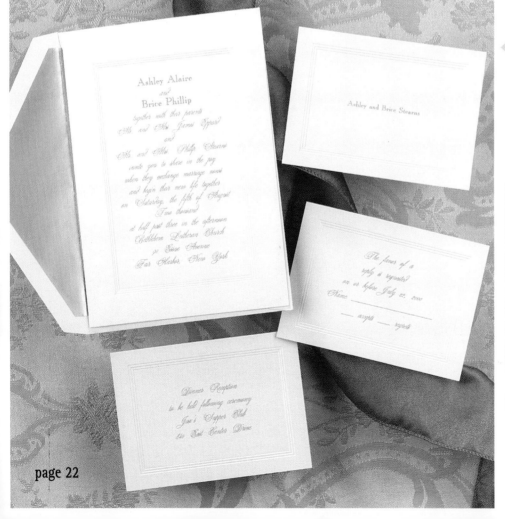

◀ CRISP PANEL

This elegant embossed triple panel card is featured on a soft white vellum. This ensemble features an informal folder. Respond and reception will be a card. 5 1/8" x 7 3/4"
WA1341-71

LINER CHOICES:

Plum, Navy, Hunter, Wine, Black, Purple, Rosewood, Silver, Taupe, Pearl, Gold, Sage, Lilac, Peach, Periwinkle, Pink, Red, Sky, Teal

ITEM	ITEM NUMBER	25	50	75
Invitation	WA1341-71	58.90	64.90	70.90
Invitation Envelope Flaps	PRTENV	22.00	23.00	26.70
Invitation Liner Envelopes	LINEDENV	4.90	9.80	14.70
Reception Cards	WAR1631	37.30	40.50	43.70
Respond Cards	WAE1631-01	45.20	49.10	53.00
Note	WAI3890-01	37.30	40.50	43.70
Note Envelope Flaps	PRTENV	22.00	23.00	26.70
Thank You Folder – Blank Inside	WAU3890-01	37.30	40.50	43.70

ITEM (cont.)	100	125	150	Add'l 25
Invitation	76.90	93.50	110.10	16.60
Invitation Envelope Flaps	30.40	34.10	37.80	3.70
Invitation Liner Envelopes	19.60	24.50	29.40	4.90
Reception Cards	46.90	56.90	66.90	10.00
Respond Cards	56.90	69.00	81.10	12.10
Note	46.90	56.90	66.90	10.00
Note Envelope Flaps	30.40	34.10	37.80	3.70
Thank You Folder – Blank Inside	46.90	56.90	66.90	10.00

ELEGANT WHITE ON WHITE

This soft white z-fold features a pearl embossed vine pattern. Your names will be printed on the front. Specify first names. The elegant satin adhesive bow is included in the price of this invitation. Customer assembly is required. 5" x 6 5/8"

WAF5631-40

LINER CHOICES:

Plum, Navy, Hunter, Wine, Black, Purple, Rosewood, Silver, Taupe, Pearl, Gold, Starlite, Aqua, Fuchsia, Lilac, Peach, Pink, Red, Royal, Sky, Teal

ITEM	ITEM NUMBER	25	50	75	100	125	150	Add'l 25
Invitation	WAF5631-40	103.00	130.30	157.60	184.90	226.80	268.70	41.90
Invitation Envelope Flaps	PRTENV	22.00	23.00	26.70	30.40	34.10	37.80	3.70
Invitation Liner Envelopes	LINEDENV	4.90	9.80	14.70	19.60	24.50	29.40	4.90
Reception Cards	WAR2563	41.50	45.30	49.10	52.90	64.20	75.50	11.30
Respond Cards	WAE2563-01	49.40	53.90	58.40	62.90	76.30	89.70	13.40
Note	WAI2563-01	41.50	45.30	49.10	52.90	64.20	75.50	11.30
Note Envelope Flaps	PRTENV	22.00	23.00	26.70	30.40	34.10	37.80	3.70
Thank You Folder – Blank Inside	WAU2563-01	41.50	45.30	49.10	52.90	64.20	75.50	11.30

SIMPLE CLASSIC SQUARE ▶

Rich bands of shimmering pearl border
this bright white square. 5 1/2" x 5 1/2"
Extra postage is required.

WA1254-37

LINER CHOICES:

Hunter, Taupe, Pearl, Gold

ITEM	ITEM NUMBER	25	50	75
Invitation	WA1254-37	81.00	90.30	99.60
Invitation Envelope Flaps	PRTENV	22.00	23.00	26.70
Invitation Liner Envelopes	LINEDENV	4.90	9.80	14.70
Reception Cards	WAR2254	40.50	44.30	48.10
Respond Cards	WAE2254-15	48.40	52.90	57.40
Note	WAI2254-15	40.50	44.30	48.10
Note Envelope Flaps	PRTENV	22.00	23.00	26.70
Thank You Folder – Blank Inside	WAU2254-15	40.50	44.30	48.10

ITEM (cont.)	100	125	150	Add'l 25
Invitation	108.90	132.30	155.70	23.40
Invitation Envelope Flaps	30.40	34.10	37.80	3.70
Invitation Liner Envelopes	19.60	24.50	29.40	4.90
Reception Cards	51.90	63.00	74.10	11.10
Respond Cards	61.90	75.10	88.30	13.20
Note	51.90	63.00	74.10	11.10
Note Envelope Flaps	30.40	34.10	37.80	3.70
Thank You Folder – Blank Inside	51.90	63.00	74.10	11.10

◀ FOREVER FLORAL

A beautiful pearl embossed heart appears on this "tea
length" bright white forever floral card. Your first
names will be printed at the top. Specify first names.
4" x 9 1/4"

WA1399-224

LINER CHOICES:

Bright Gold, Taupe, Pearl

ITEM	ITEM NUMBER	25	50	75
Invitation	WA1399-224	95.90	106.90	117.90
Invitation Envelope Flaps	PRTENV	22.00	23.00	26.70
Invitation Liner Envelopes	LINEDENV	4.90	9.80	14.70
Reception Cards	WAR2399	43.60	47.70	51.80
Respond Cards	WAE2399-27	51.50	56.30	61.10
Note	WAI2399-27	43.60	47.70	51.80
Note Envelope Flaps	PRTENV	22.00	23.00	26.70
Thank You Folder – Blank Inside	WAU2399-27	43.60	47.70	51.80

ITEM (cont.)	100	125	150	Add'l 25
Invitation	128.90	156.50	184.10	27.60
Invitation Envelope Flaps	30.40	34.10	37.80	3.70
Invitation Liner Envelopes	19.60	24.50	29.40	4.90
Reception Cards	55.90	67.80	79.70	11.90
Respond Cards	65.90	80.00	94.10	14.10
Note	55.90	67.80	79.70	11.90
Note Envelope Flaps	30.40	34.10	37.80	3.70
Thank You Folder – Blank Inside	55.90	67.80	79.70	11.90

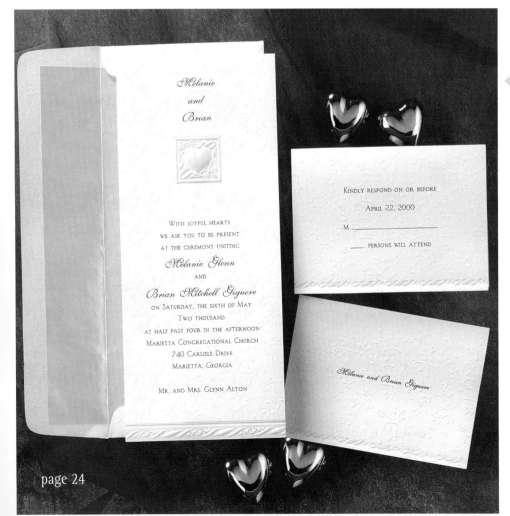

▷ ROMANTIC GLOW

Shimmering pearl bands richly sculpture this bright white square. 7" x 7"
Extra postage is required.
WA923-68

LINER CHOICES:

Wine, Black, Purple, Rosewood, Silver, Taupe, Pearl, Gold, Periwinkle, Pink, Teal, Peach, Sky, Starlite

ITEM	ITEM NUMBER	25	50	75
Invitation	WA923-68	97.00	108.30	119.60
Invitation Envelope Flaps	PRTENV	22.00	23.00	26.70
Invitation Liner Envelopes	LINEDENV	4.90	9.80	14.70
Reception Cards	WAR9230	41.50	45.30	49.10
Respond Cards	WAE9230-15	49.40	53.90	58.40
Note	WAI9230-15	41.50	45.30	49.10
Note Envelope Flaps	PRTENV	22.00	23.00	26.70
Thank You Folder – Blank Inside	WAU9230-15	41.50	45.30	49.10

ITEM (cont.)	100	125	150	Add'l 25
Invitation	130.90	158.90	186.90	28.00
Invitation Envelope Flaps	30.40	34.10	37.80	3.70
Invitation Liner Envelopes	19.60	24.50	29.40	4.90
Reception Cards	52.90	64.20	75.50	11.30
Respond Cards	62.90	76.30	89.70	13.40
Note	52.90	64.20	75.50	11.30
Note Envelope Flaps	30.40	34.10	37.80	3.70
Thank You Folder – Blank Inside	52.90	64.20	75.50	11.30

SOPHISTICATED FLOURISH ▷

This bright white square is highlighted with pearl embossed flourishes around the border. 7" x 7"
Extra postage is required.
WA8052-68

LINER CHOICES:

Wine, Black, Purple, Rosewood, Silver, Taupe, Pearl, Gold, Periwinkle, Pink, Teal

ITEM	ITEM NUMBER	25	50	75
Invitation	WA8052-68	96.40	107.90	119.40
Invitation Envelope Flaps	PRTENV	22.00	23.00	26.70
Invitation Liner Envelopes	LINEDENV	4.90	9.80	14.70
Reception Cards	WAR2258	40.50	44.30	48.10
Respond Cards	WAE2258-15	48.40	52.90	57.40
Note	WAI2258-15	40.50	44.30	48.10
Note Envelope Flaps	PRTENV	22.00	23.00	26.70
Thank You Folder – Blank Inside	WAU2258-15	40.50	44.30	48.10

ITEM (cont.)	100	125	150	Add'l 25
Invitation	130.90	158.90	186.90	28.00
Invitation Envelope Flaps	30.40	34.10	37.80	3.70
Invitation Liner Envelopes	19.60	24.50	29.40	4.90
Reception Cards	51.90	63.00	74.10	11.10
Respond Cards	61.90	75.10	88.30	13.20
Note	51.90	63.00	74.10	11.10
Note Envelope Flaps	30.40	34.10	37.80	3.70
Thank You Folder – Blank Inside	51.90	63.00	74.10	11.10

I DO ▶

Two youngsters share tender moments on the front of this white z-fold invitation. The brown-tone portraits are highlighted by a red rose and preprinted gold foil wording; He asked ... She said "Yes!" which follows through inside with the caption; They'll say "I do!" 5" x 6 5/8"

WA4481-40

LINER CHOICES:

Hunter, Wine, Black, Rosewood, Pearl, Gold, Pink, Red

ITEM	ITEM NUMBER	25	50	75
Invitation	WA4481-40	100.60	112.70	124.80
Invitation Envelope Flaps	PRTENV	22.00	23.00	26.70
Invitation Liner Envelopes	LINEDENV	4.90	9.80	14.70
Reception Cards	WAR2480	43.50	47.30	51.10
Respond Cards	WAE2480-01	51.40	55.90	60.40
Note	WAI2480-01	43.50	47.30	51.10
Note Envelope Flaps	PRTENV	22.00	23.00	26.70
Thank You Folder – Blank Inside	WAU2480-01	43.50	47.30	51.10

ITEM (cont.)	100	125	150	Add'l 25
Invitation	136.90	166.20	195.50	29.30
Invitation Envelope Flaps	30.40	34.10	37.80	3.70
Invitation Liner Envelopes	19.60	24.50	29.40	4.90
Reception Cards	54.90	66.60	78.30	11.70
Respond Cards	64.90	78.70	92.50	13.80
Note	54.90	66.60	78.30	11.70
Note Envelope Flaps	30.40	34.10	37.80	3.70
Thank You Folder – Blank Inside	54.90	66.60	78.30	11.70

◀ ONE LOVE

A simple, but elegant design with interlocking gold stemmed white roses on a translucent short z-fold. For a personal touch, your names and a quotation of your choice appear on the front of this invitation, please specify names. Silver and other light ink colors are not recommended. When writing on translucent paper, permanent pen is recommended to prevent smearing. 5" x 6 5/8"

WA6651-40

LINER CHOICES:

Plum, Navy, Hunter, Wine, Black, Purple, Rosewood, Silver, Taupe, Pearl, Gold, Aqua, Fuchsia, Lilac, Peach, Pink, Red, Royal, Sky, Starlite, Teal

ITEM	ITEM NUMBER	25	50	75
Invitation	WA6651-40	105.50	117.30	129.10
Invitation Envelope Flaps	PRTENV	22.00	23.00	26.70
Invitation Liner Envelopes	LINEDENV	4.90	9.80	14.70
Reception Cards	WAR2566	45.00	49.30	53.60
Respond Cards	WAE2566-01	52.90	57.90	62.90
Note	WAI2566-01	45.00	49.30	53.60
Note Envelope Flaps	PRTENV	22.00	23.00	26.70
Thank You Folder – Blank Inside	WAU2566-01	45.00	49.30	53.60

ITEM (cont.)	100	125	150	Add'l 25
Invitation	140.90	170.80	200.70	29.90
Invitation Envelope Flaps	30.40	34.10	37.80	3.70
Invitation Liner Envelopes	19.60	24.50	29.40	4.90
Reception Cards	57.90	70.30	82.70	12.40
Respond Cards	67.90	82.40	96.90	14.50
Note	57.90	70.30	82.70	12.40
Note Envelope Flaps	30.40	34.10	37.80	3.70
Thank You Folder – Blank Inside	57.90	70.30	82.70	12.40

GARDEN-FRESH FLOWERS

This lavish, bright white square card features a flourish of vivid flowers printed on the border. Your invitation wording is surrounded by the floral border. Due to the generous size of this invitation, additional postage is required. 7" x 7"

WA5841-68

LINER CHOICES:

Black, Gold, Pearl, Periwinkle, Pink, Purple, Rosewood, Silver, Sky, Taupe, Teal, Wine

ITEM	ITEM NUMBER	25	50	75	100	125	150	Add'l 25
Invitation	WA5841-68	97.80	109.50	121.20	132.90	161.40	189.90	28.50
Invitation Envelope Flaps	PRTENV	22.00	23.00	26.70	30.40	34.10	37.80	3.70
Invitation Liner Envelopes	LINEDENV	4.90	9.80	14.70	19.60	24.50	29.40	4.90
Reception Cards	WAR7084	45.60	49.70	53.80	57.90	70.30	82.70	12.40
Respond Cards	WAE7084-15	54.50	59.30	64.10	68.90	83.60	98.30	14.70
Note	WAI7084-15	45.60	49.70	53.80	57.90	70.30	82.70	12.40
Note Envelope Flaps	PRTENV	22.00	23.00	26.70	30.40	34.10	37.80	3.70
Thank You Folder – Blank Inside	WAU7084-15	45.60	49.70	53.80	57.90	70.30	82.70	12.40

...TUMN HUES

...utumn array of leaves and trees adorn the front and inside panels of this ecru z-fold ...tion. Your first names and wedding date will be printed on the front. Please specify first ...s and wedding date. The invitation opens to showcase a quotation of your choice in the ...r and your invitation wording will be printed flush left on the right panel. 5" x 6 5/8"

...871-40

...ER CHOICES:

...Black, Hunter, Pearl, Taupe, Wine

	ITEM NUMBER	25	50	75	100	125	150	Add'l 25
...ion	WA5871-40	100.60	112.70	124.80	136.90	166.20	195.50	29.30
...ion Envelope Flaps	PRTENV	22.00	23.00	26.70	30.40	34.10	37.80	3.70
...ion Liner Envelopes	LINEDENV	4.90	9.80	14.70	19.60	24.50	29.40	4.90
...ion Cards	WAR7871	43.50	47.30	51.10	54.90	66.60	78.30	11.70
...d Cards	WAE7871-01	51.40	55.90	60.40	64.90	78.70	92.50	13.80
	WAI7871-01	43.50	47.30	51.10	54.90	66.60	78.30	11.70
...nvelope Flaps	PRTENV	22.00	23.00	26.70	30.40	34.10	37.80	3.70
...You Folder ...k Inside	WAU7871-01	43.50	47.30	51.10	54.90	66.60	78.30	11.70

SONG OF CELEBRATION

You are celebrating your love and the start of your new life. The swirling wording; "This Day I Will Marry My Friend" in silver foil accents the cutaway heart. Behind the heart is an array of pastel colors which opens to display your invitation wording. 5" x 6 5/8"

WA5873-40

LINER CHOICES:

Aqua, Black, Gold, Hunter, Lilac, Pearl, Pink, Purple, Rosewood, Silver, Teal

ITEM	ITEM NUMBER	25	50	75	100	125	150	Add'l 25
Invitation	WA5873-40	107.90	120.90	133.90	146.90	178.30	209.70	31.40
Invitation Envelope Flaps	PRTENV	22.00	23.00	26.70	30.40	34.10	37.80	3.70
Invitation Liner Envelopes	LINEDENV	4.90	9.80	14.70	19.60	24.50	29.40	4.90
Reception Cards	WAR7873	43.50	47.30	51.10	54.90	66.60	78.30	11.70
Respond Cards	WAE7873-01	51.40	55.90	60.40	64.90	78.70	92.50	13.80
Note	WAI7873-01	43.50	47.30	51.10	54.90	66.60	78.30	11.70
Note Envelope Flaps	PRTENV	22.00	23.00	26.70	30.40	34.10	37.80	3.70
Thank You Folder – Blank Inside	WAU7873-01	43.50	47.30	51.10	54.90	66.60	78.30	11.70

ALL THE TRIMMINGS ▶

This bright white, forever floral paper is a symbol of eternal love. The cut out heart, with a delicate chiffon ribbon pulled through the heart opening, gives a unique feeling of romance. Your first names and wedding date appear on the bottom of the invitation. Please specify first names and wedding date. A two-line quotation of your choice is printed above your names to add to the invitation's charm and speaks volumes about your love and who you are. 5" x 6 5/8"
WAF5902-49

LINER CHOICES:

Pearl, Bright Gold

ITEM	ITEM NUMBER	25	50	75
Invitation	WAF5902-49	117.80	131.50	145.20
Invitation Envelope Flaps	PRTENV	22.00	23.00	26.70
Invitation Liner Envelopes	LINEDENV	4.90	9.80	14.70
Reception Cards	WAR7090	45.60	49.70	53.80
Respond Cards	WAE7090-27	54.50	59.30	64.10
Note	WAI7090-27	45.60	49.70	53.80
Note Envelope Flaps	PRTENV	22.00	23.00	26.70
Thank You Folder – Blank Inside	WAU7090-27	45.60	49.70	53.80

ITEM (cont.)	100	125	150	Add'l 25
Invitation	158.90	192.90	226.90	34.00
Invitation Envelope Flaps	30.40	34.10	37.80	3.70
Invitation Liner Envelopes	19.60	24.50	29.40	4.90
Reception Cards	57.90	70.30	82.70	12.40
Respond Cards	68.90	83.60	98.30	14.70
Note	57.90	70.30	82.70	12.40
Note Envelope Flaps	30.40	34.10	37.80	3.70
Thank You Folder – Blank Inside	57.90	70.30	82.70	12.40

◀ COLORFUL TREASURE

Your invitation wording is printed amidst soft pink and white stripes. A pretty translucent overlay with roses folds around your base card and is sure to capture the hearts of your guests! Customer assembly is required. 5 1/8" x 7 1/4"
WAN5903-71

LINER CHOICES:

Rosewood, Black, Gold, Hunter, Pearl, Pink, Plum, Sage, Teal

ITEM	ITEM NUMBER	25	50	75
Invitation	WAN5903-71	123.40	137.90	152.40
Invitation Envelope Flaps	PRTENV	22.00	23.00	26.70
Invitation Liner Envelopes	LINEDENV	4.90	9.80	14.70
Reception Cards	WANR7903	47.00	51.30	55.60
Respond Cards	WANE7903-01	54.90	59.90	64.90
Note	WANI7903-01	47.00	51.30	55.60
Note Envelope Flaps	PRTENV	22.00	23.00	26.70
Thank You Folder – Blank Inside	NA	47.00	51.30	55.60

ITEM (cont.)	100	125	150	Add'l 25
Invitation	166.90	202.60	238.30	35.70
Invitation Envelope Flaps	30.40	34.10	37.80	3.70
Invitation Liner Envelopes	19.60	24.50	29.40	4.90
Reception Cards	59.90	72.70	85.50	12.80
Respond Cards	69.90	84.80	99.70	14.90
Note	59.90	72.70	85.50	12.80
Note Envelope Flaps	30.40	34.10	37.80	3.70
Thank You Folder – Blank Inside	59.90	72.70	85.50	12.80

2 LIVES 1 LOVE

A white z-fold features sterling silver wording; "2 Lives Be Come 1 Love" Your first names appear on the front; open to your last names and invitation wording inside over the sterling silver wording. This is truly a unique invitation and gives the feeling of romance. Due to the unique design of this invitation, the invitation wording is only available as shown. The invitation wording will be sampled after your wedding profile information. 4" x 9 1/4"

WA5894-223

LINER CHOICES:

Black, Bright Gold, Pearl, Sage, Taupe

ITEM	ITEM NUMBER	25	50	75	100	125	150	Add'l 25
Invitation	WA5894-223	126.90	142.90	158.90	174.90	212.30	249.70	37.40
Invitation Envelope Flaps	PRTENV	22.00	23.00	26.70	30.40	34.10	37.80	3.70
Invitation Liner Envelopes	LINEDENV	4.90	9.80	14.70	19.60	24.50	29.40	4.90
Reception Cards	WAR7894	43.50	47.30	51.10	54.90	66.60	78.30	11.70
Respond Cards	WAE7894-15	51.40	55.90	60.40	64.90	78.90	92.50	13.80
Note	WAI7894-15	43.50	47.30	51.10	54.90	66.60	78.30	11.70
Note Envelope Flaps	PRTENV	22.00	23.00	26.70	30.40	34.10	37.80	3.70
Thank You Folder – Blank Inside	WAU7894-15	43.50	47.30	51.10	54.90	66.60	78.30	11.70

STAR CROSSED LOVERS ▶

Your invitation wording is revealed when you open the white window. The translucent stars and hearts are tied to the window cut out with a delicate, white chiffon ribbon. Customer assembly is required. 5" x 6 5/8"

WAN5896-40

LINER CHOICES:

Wine, Aqua, Black, Fuchsia, Gold, Hunter, Lilac, Navy, Peach, Pearl, Pink, Plum, Purple, Red, Rosewood, Royal Blue, Silver, Sky, Starlite, Taupe, Teal

ITEM	ITEM NUMBER	25	50	75	100	125	150	Add'l 25
Invitation	WAN5896-40	123.40	137.90	152.40	166.90	202.60	238.30	35.70
Invitation Envelope Flaps	PRTENV	22.00	23.00	26.70	30.40	34.10	37.80	3.70
Invitation Liner Envelopes	LINEDENV	4.90	9.80	14.70	19.60	24.50	29.40	4.90
Reception Cards	WAR7896	39.30	42.50	45.70	48.90	59.40	69.90	10.50
Respond Cards	WAE7896-01	47.20	51.10	55.00	58.90	71.50	84.10	12.60
Note	WAI7896-01	39.30	42.50	45.70	48.90	59.40	69.90	10.50
Note Envelope Flaps	PRTENV	22.00	23.00	26.70	30.40	34.10	37.80	3.70
Thank You Folder – Blank Inside	WAU7896-01	39.30	42.50	45.70	48.90	59.40	69.90	10.50

WHIMSICAL PERIWINKLE

A band of periwinkle flowers border the edge of this bright white card. A soft periwinkle tinted overlay covers your invitation wording with sheer beauty. The two layers are tied together with delicate sheer white ribbon. Customer assembly is required. 5 3/8" x 7 3/4"

WAN0901-87

LINER CHOICES:

Black, Pearl, Periwinkle, Purple, Silver

ITEM	ITEM NUMBER	25	50	75	100	125	150	Add'l 25
Invitation	WAN0901-87	131.10	147.70	164.30	180.90	219.60	258.30	38.70
Invitation Envelope Flaps	PRTENV	22.00	23.00	26.70	30.40	34.10	37.80	3.70
Invitation Liner Envelopes	LINEDENV	4.90	9.80	14.70	19.60	24.50	29.40	4.90
Reception Cards	WAR7901	45.60	49.70	53.80	57.90	70.30	82.70	12.40
Respond Cards	WAE7901-15	54.50	59.30	64.10	68.90	83.60	98.30	14.70
Note	WAI7901-15	45.60	49.70	53.80	57.90	70.30	82.70	12.40
Note Envelope Flaps	PRTENV	22.00	23.00	26.70	30.40	34.10	37.80	3.70
Thank You Folder – Blank Inside	WAU7901-15	45.60	49.70	53.80	57.90	70.30	82.70	12.40

WRAPPED IN ELEGANCE (WHITE) ▶

A sheet of translucent white paper is printed with your first names to form an elegant wrap for the bright white, non-folding invitation card inside. Your names are printed in the same lettering and ink color as your wording, which is printed on the inside card. Please specify names; if not specified, we will use the first names from the invitation wording.

ON THE INVITATION:
Lettering Style #160
Black Ink
Printed Return Envelope

LINER CHOICES:
Aqua, Black (shown), Burgundy, Gold, Hunter, Lilac,
Navy, Peach, Pearl, Periwinkle, Pink, Purple, Red,
Rosewood, Silver, Taupe, Teal, Wedgewood
SIZE: 5 1/8" x 7 5/16"

ITEM	ITEM NUMBER	25	50	75	100	125	150	Add'l 25
Invitation	0IA-KIT13W	95.90	104.90	113.90	122.90	151.20	179.50	28.30
Printed Invitation Envelope Flaps	0IA-VBWJO	22.90	26.90	28.90	30.90	35.40	39.90	4.50
Lined Inner Envelopes	Specify Color	4.90	9.80	14.70	19.60	24.50	29.40	4.90
Reception Folder	0IA-F9160R	32.90	34.90	36.90	38.90	47.50	56.10	8.60
Respond Folder	0IA-F9160E	40.90	42.90	44.90	46.90	57.30	67.70	10.40
Informal Notes	0IA-F9160N	32.90	34.90	36.90	38.90	47.50	56.10	8.60
Thank You Folder – Blank Inside	0IA-F9160T	32.90	34.90	36.90	38.90	47.50	56.10	8.60
Thank You Folder – Printed Inside	0IA-F9160T2	53.40	55.40	63.60	71.80	86.60	101.40	14.80
Printed Envelope Flaps	0IA-VBW200	22.90	26.90	28.90	30.90	35.40	39.90	4.50

WRAPPED IN ELEGANCE (ECRU)

A sheet of translucent ecru paper is printed with your first names to form an elegant wrap for the ecru non-folding invitation card inside. Your names are printed in the same lettering and ink color as your wording, which is printed on the inside card. Please specify names; if not specified, we will use the first names from the invitation

ON THE INVITATION:
Lettering Style #074
Gold Ink

LINER CHOICES:
Gold (shown), Pearl, Taupe
SIZE: 5 1/8" x 7 5/16"

ITEM	ITEM NUMBER	25	50	75	100	125	150	Add'l 25
Invitation	0IA-KIT03W	95.90	104.90	113.90	122.90	151.20	179.50	28.30
Printed Invitation Envelope Flaps	0IA-ERJO	22.90	26.90	28.90	30.90	35.40	39.90	4.50
Lined Inner Envelopes	Specify Color	4.90	9.80	14.70	19.60	24.50	29.40	4.90
Reception Folder	0IA-W8888R	35.90	37.90	39.90	41.90	51.10	60.30	9.20
Respond Folder	0IA-W8888E	43.90	45.90	47.90	49.90	60.90	71.90	11.00
Informal Notes	0IA-W401N	35.90	37.90	39.90	41.90	51.10	60.30	9.20
Thank You Folder – Blank Inside	0IA-W401T	35.90	37.90	39.90	41.90	51.10	60.30	9.20
Thank You Folder – Printed Inside	0IA-W401T2	56.40	58.40	66.60	74.80	90.20	105.60	15.40
Printed Envelope Flaps	0IA-ER200	22.90	26.90	28.90	30.90	35.40	39.90	4.50

PANELS OF PEARL ▶

A bright white folded invitation is bordered with embossed panels, adding dimension to your wording on the front. Two bands of pearl foil add unforgettable luster. Invitations include tissues, unlined inner envelopes and blank outer envelopes. Respond folders include printed return envelopes. Note paper and thank you note folders include blank envelopes. Prices are for black ink. For a colorful ink, add $7.00 to the total price of each printed item.

ON THE INVITATION:
Lettering Style #238
Black Ink

LINER CHOICES:
Aqua, Black (shown), Burgundy, Gold, Hunter, Lilac, Navy,
Peach, Pearl, Periwinkle, Pink, Purple, Red, Rosewood, Silver,
Taupe, Teal, Wedgewood
SIZE: 5 1/8" x 7 5/16"

ITEM	ITEM NUMBER	25	50	75	100	125	150	Add'l 25
Invitation	0IA-W559W	82.90	91.90	100.90	108.90	134.00	159.10	25.10
Printed Invitation Envelope Flaps	0IA-VBWJO	22.90	26.90	28.90	30.90	35.40	39.90	4.50
Lined Inner Envelopes	Specify Color	4.90	9.80	14.70	19.60	24.50	29.40	4.90
Reception Folder	0IA-W8790R	46.90	48.90	50.90	52.90	64.50	76.10	11.60
Respond Folder	0IA-W8790E	54.90	56.90	58.90	60.90	74.30	87.70	13.40
Informal Notes	0IA-W8790N	46.90	48.90	50.90	52.90	64.50	76.10	11.60
Thank You Folder – Blank Inside	0IA-W8790T	46.90	48.90	50.90	52.90	64.50	76.10	11.60
Thank You Folder – Printed Inside	0IA-W8790T2	67.40	69.40	77.60	85.80	103.60	121.40	17.80
Printed Envelope Flaps	0IA-VBW200	22.90	26.90	28.90	30.90	35.40	39.90	4.50

◀ EPICAL ROMANCE

Absolutely stunning...this pink and white tea length invitation sets off the elegant sterling silver flourishes. A delicate, petite chiffon bow combines to create a wedding invitation of breathtaking beauty. Please specify first names for the front of the invitation. Customer assembly is required. 4" x 9 1/4"

WAF5916-223

LINER CHOICES:

Pearl, Black, Bright Gold

ITEM	ITEM NUMBER	25	50	75
Invitation	WAF5916-223	144.90	178.90	212.90
Invitation Envelope Flaps	PRTENV	22.00	23.00	26.70
Invitation Liner Envelopes	LINEDENV	4.90	9.80	14.70
Reception Cards	WAR7916	45.60	49.70	53.80
Respond Cards	WAE7916-15	54.50	59.30	64.10
Note	WAI7916-15	45.60	49.70	53.80
Note Envelope Flaps	PRTENV	22.00	23.00	26.70
Thank You Folder – Blank Inside	WAU7916-15	45.60	49.70	53.80

ITEM (cont.)	100	125	150	Add'l 25
Invitation	246.90	302.30	357.70	55.40
Invitation Envelope Flaps	30.40	34.10	37.80	3.70
Invitation Liner Envelopes	19.60	24.50	29.40	4.90
Reception Cards	57.90	70.30	82.70	12.40
Respond Cards	68.90	83.60	98.30	14.70
Note	57.90	70.30	82.70	12.40
Note Envelope Flaps	30.40	34.10	37.80	3.70
Thank You Folder – Blank Inside	57.90	70.30	82.70	12.40

WATERCOLOR PASTELS ▶

This bright white tea length folder is wrapped within a floral watercolor translucent wrap. The wrap softly folds over your invitation wording inside the folder. A bright white name card with your first names is tied to this invitation with a delicate white chiffon ribbon. Customer assembly is required. Please specify your first names. When writing on translucent paper, permanent pen is recommended to prevent smearing. 4" x 9 1/2"

WAN5915-223

LINER CHOICES:

Black, Bright Gold, Pearl, Sage

ITEM	ITEM NUMBER	25	50	75
Invitation	WAN5915-223	183.00	218.30	253.60
Invitation Envelope Flaps	PRTENV	22.00	23.00	26.70
Invitation Liner Envelopes	LINEDENV	4.90	9.80	14.70
Reception Cards	WAR7915	47.00	51.30	55.60
Respond Cards	WAE7915-15	54.90	59.90	64.90
Note	WAI7915-15	47.00	51.30	55.60
Note Envelope Flaps	PRTENV	22.00	23.00	26.70
Thank You Folder – Blank Inside	WAU7915-15	47.00	51.30	55.60

ITEM (cont.)	100	125	150	Add'l 25
Invitation	288.90	350.50	412.10	61.60
Invitation Envelope Flaps	30.40	34.10	37.80	3.70
Invitation Liner Envelopes	19.60	24.50	29.40	4.90
Reception Cards	59.90	72.70	85.50	12.80
Respond Cards	69.90	84.80	99.70	14.90
Note	59.90	72.70	85.50	12.80
Note Envelope Flaps	30.40	34.10	37.80	3.70
Thank You Folder – Blank Inside	59.90	72.70	85.50	12.80

ORDER ONLINE AT:
YourBridalSuperstore.com

CELEBRATION ▶

Start your special celebration with this elegant square invitation. Bands of pearl foil border this large, non-folding card of thick, bright white paper. Because of the unique size and shape of this invitation, extra postage is required. Invitations include tissues, unlined inner envelopes and blank outer envelopes. Respond folders include printed return envelopes. Note paper and thank you note folders include blank envelopes. Prices are for black ink. For a colorful ink, add $7.00 to the total price of each printed item.

ON THE INVITATION:	LINER CHOICES:
Lettering Style #014	Black, Dark Blue, Gold,
Black Ink	Pearl (shown), Periwinkle,
Printed Return Envelope	Pink, Purple, Silver, Teal
	SIZE: 7" x 7"

ITEM	ITEM NUMBER	25	50	75
Invitation	OIA-356WH	60.90	66.90	72.90
Printed Invitation Envelope Flaps	OIA-ERJO	22.90	26.90	28.90
Lined Inner Envelopes	Specify Color	4.90	9.80	14.70
Reception Folder	OIA-7905R	40.90	42.90	44.90
Respond Folder	OIA-7905E	48.90	50.90	52.90
Informal Notes	OIA-7905N	40.90	42.90	44.90
Thank You Folder – Blank Inside	OIA-7905T	40.90	42.90	44.90
Thank You Folder – Printed Inside	OIA-7905T2	61.40	63.40	69.60
Printed Envelope Flaps	OIA-ER200	22.90	26.90	28.90

ITEM (cont.)	100	125	150	Add'l 25
Invitation	78.90	97.10	115.30	18.20
Printed Invitation Envelope Flaps	30.90	35.40	39.90	4.50
Lined Inner Envelopes	19.60	24.50	29.40	4.90
Reception Folder	46.90	57.20	67.50	10.30
Respond Folder	54.90	67.00	79.10	12.10
Informal Notes	46.90	57.20	67.50	10.30
Thank You Folder – Blank Inside	46.90	57.20	67.50	10.30
Thank You Folder – Printed Inside	75.80	82.00	88.20	6.20
Printed Envelope Flaps	30.90	35.40	39.90	4.50

WISPS OF WATERCOLOR

Soft strokes of yellow, purple, fuchsia and hunter watercolors have created the romantic little flowers that crown this bright white folded invitation. Your wording is printed beneath the floral design on the front. Invitations include tissues, unlined inner envelopes and blank outer envelopes. Respond folders include printed return envelopes. Note paper and thank you note folders include blank envelopes. Prices are for black ink. For a colorful ink, add $7.00

ON THE INVITATION:	LINER CHOICES:
Lettering Style #337	Black, Gold, Hunter,
Purple Ink	Lilac, Pearl, Periwinkle,
	Purple (shown), Rosewood,
	Silver, Taupe
	SIZE: 5 1/8" x 7 5/16"

ITEM	ITEM NUMBER	25	50	75
Invitation	OIA-W2314W	72.90	80.90	88.90
Printed Invitation Envelope Flaps	OIA-VBWJO	22.90	26.90	28.90
Lined Inner Envelopes	Spec. Color	4.90	9.80	14.70
Reception Folder	OIA-W2314R	43.90	45.90	47.90
Respond Folder	OIA-W2314E	51.90	53.90	55.90
Informal Notes	OIA-W2314N	43.90	45.90	47.90
Thank You Folder – Blank Inside	OIA-W2314T	43.90	45.90	47.90
Thank You Folder – Printed Inside	OIA-W2314T2	64.40	66.40	74.60
Printed Envelope Flaps	OIA-VBW200	22.90	26.90	28.90

ITEM (cont.)	100	125	150	Add'l 25
Invitation	96.90	119.20	141.50	22.30
Printed Invitation Envelope Flaps	30.90	35.40	39.90	4.50
Lined Inner Envelopes	19.60	24.50	29.40	4.90
Reception Folder	49.90	60.90	71.90	11.00
Respond Folder	57.90	70.70	83.50	12.80
Informal Notes	49.90	60.90	71.90	11.00
Thank You Folder – Blank Inside	49.90	60.90	71.90	11.00
Thank You Folder – Printed Inside	82.80	100.00	117.20	17.20
Printed Envelope Flaps	30.90	35.40	39.90	4.50

2435 Carol Court
Broad Acres, Michigan 48035

A fresh new day, and it is ours

a day of happy beginnings

when we, Jenna Marie Tanner

and Tyler John Stevenson

pledge our love as one

on Saturday, the twelfth of May

two thousand and one

at two o'clock in the afternoon

Hosanna Lutheran Church

105 Hosanna Avenue

Broad Acres, Michigan

We joyfully ask you

to share this day with us

The favor of a reply is requested

on or before April 28, 2001

M _____

_____ persons will attend

Miss Jenna Tanner

2435 Carol Court

Broad Acres, Michigan 48035

Jenna and Tyler
May 12, 2001

M _____

Table No. _____

DAISY MEADOW

Daisies "spring" from the embossed border of this large ecru invitation – lending pretty freshness to weddings held any time of year! Lined inner envelopes available: gold (shown), hunter, pearl, rosewood and wine. Displayed with wording W132 in gold ink and lettering style BIC

SIZE: 5 1/2" x 7 3/4"

ITEM	ITEM #	25	50	75	100	Add'l 25
Invitation	WFU855	92.90	94.90	96.90	98.90	21.00
Informal Note	WF8551	43.90	44.90	45.90	46.90	10.00
Reception	WF8553	43.90	44.90	45.90	46.90	10.00
Respond	WF8554	53.90	54.90	55.90	56.90	12.20
Printed Outer Envelopes	PENV	22.00	23.00	26.70	30.40	3.70
Lined Inner Envelopes	LENV	4.90	9.80	14.70	19.60	4.90

Pricing includes black raised lettering and 14 lines of wording. For colored inks, add $7.00 to the TOTAL price of each item. Additional lines are $1.50 each.

ORDER ONLINE AT:
YourBridalSuperstore.com

PEACEFUL BLISS ▸

"From this Day Forward," that meaningful, promise-filled phrase from traditional wedding vows, is featured in glistening gold script on the front of these ecru invitations. The words are surrounded by a heart-shaped border complete with ribbons, roses and doves in flight. Your wording appears when the invitation is opened. Lined inner envelope available: gold. Displayed with wording W17 in gold ink and lettering style FLS.

SIZE: 4 1/2" x 5 7/8"

ITEM	ITEM #	25	50	75	100	Add'l 25
Invitation	WFD352	60.90	62.90	64.90	66.90	14.20
Informal Note	WF0351	43.90	44.90	45.90	46.90	10.00
Reception	WF0353	43.90	44.90	45.90	46.90	10.00
Respond	WF0354	53.90	54.90	55.90	56.90	12.20
Printed Outer Envelopes	PENV	22.00	23.00	26.70	30.40	3.70
Lined Inner Envelopes	LENV	4.90	9.80	14.70	19.60	4.90

Pricing includes black raised lettering and 14 lines of wording. For colored inks, add $7.00 to the TOTAL price of each item. Additional lines are $1.50 each.

ANGEL ECHOES

Playful cherubs, classic columns and roses lend a touch of tender Victorian charm to this soft white invitation. The design is embossed to add romantic dimension to your wording. Available lined inner envelope colors: black, blue, gold, hunter, lilac, navy, peach, pearl, periwinkle, pink, plum, purple, red, rosewood (shown), sage, silver, taupe, teal and wine. Displayed with wording W36 in rosewood ink.

SIZE: 5 1/8" x 7 1/4"

ITEM	ITEM #	25	50	75	100	Add'l 25
Invitation	WFJ474	74.90	76.90	78.90	80.90	17.20
Informal Note	WF4741	43.90	44.90	45.90	46.90	10.00
Reception	WF4743	43.90	44.90	45.90	46.90	10.00
Respond	WF4744	53.90	54.90	55.90	56.90	12.20
Printed Outer Envelopes	PENV	22.00	23.00	26.70	30.40	3.70
Lined Inner Envelopes	LENV	4.90	9.80	14.70	19.60	4.90

Pricing includes black raised lettering and 14 lines of wording. For colored inks, add $7.00 to the TOTAL price of each item. Additional lines are $1.50 each.

PRISTINE CALLA LILIES ▸

Majestic, perfectly formed calla lilies surround your wording on the front of this bright white invitation card. The lilies are embossed for dramatic dimension. Lined inner envelopes available: black, gold (shown), hunter, peach, pearl, periwinkle, pink, plum, purple, rosewood, sage, silver, taupe, teal and wine. Displayed with wording W45 in gold ink and lettering style FNH.

SIZE: 5 1/2" x 7 3/4"

ITEM	ITEM #	25	50	75	100	Add'l 25
Invitation	WFU513	124.90	126.90	128.90	130.90	27.80
Informal Note	WF5131	49.90	50.90	51.90	52.90	11.20
Reception	WF5133	49.90	50.90	51.90	52.90	11.20
Respond	WF5134	59.90	60.90	61.90	62.90	13.40
Printed Outer Envelopes	PENV	22.00	23.00	26.70	30.40	3.70
Lined Inner Envelopes	LENV	4.90	9.80	14.70	19.60	4.90

Pricing includes black raised lettering and 14 lines of wording. For colored inks, add $7.00 to the TOTAL price of each item. Additional lines are $1.50 each.

▲ SWIRL OF ROMANCE

Swirling vines and filigree in striking silver foil make this invitation irresistibly elegant! The bright white paper also features a striped border to beautifully frame your wording on the front. Lined inner envelopes available: black, hunter, peach, pearl, periwinkle, pink, plum, purple, rosewood, sage, silver, taupe, teal and wine. Displayed with wording W14 in silver ink.

SIZE: 5 1/2" x 7 3/4"

ITEM	ITEM #	25	50	75	100	Add'l 25
Invitation	WFU455	116.90	118.90	120.90	122.90	26.10
Informal Note	WF4551	52.90	53.90	54.90	55.90	11.90
Reception	WF4553	52.90	53.90	54.90	55.90	11.90
Respond	WF4554	62.90	63.90	64.90	65.90	14.10
Printed Outer Envelopes	PENV	22.00	23.00	26.70	30.40	3.70
Lined Inner Envelopes	LENV	4.90	9.80	14.70	19.60	4.90

Pricing includes black raised lettering and 14 lines of wording. For colored inks, add $7.00 to the TOTAL price of each item. Additional lines are $1.50 each.

ROMANCE ▶

A-B) A perfect long-stemmed rose, complete with a tiny bud, is embossed to accent your wording. The invitation is available in your choice of creamy ecru (A) or soft white (B) paper to match the tone and the color scheme of your wedding. Lined inner envelopes available for ecru (A): gold, hunter, pearl and wine. Shown with wording W36 in black ink and typestyle PA. Lined inner envelopes for soft white (B): black, blue, fuchsia, gold, hunter (shown), lilac, navy, peach, pearl, pink, plum, purple, red, rosewood, silver, teal and wine. Displayed with wording W132 in hunter ink and lettering style SRH.

SIZE: 5" x 6 5/8"

Ecru (A)

ITEM	ITEM #	25	50	75	100	Add'l 25
Invitation	WFE195	65.90	67.90	69.90	71.90	15.30
Informal Note	WF1951	43.90	44.90	45.90	46.90	10.00
Reception	WF1953	43.90	44.90	45.90	46.90	10.00
Respond	WF1954	53.90	54.90	55.90	56.90	12.20
Printed Outer Envelopes	PENV	22.00	23.00	26.70	30.40	3.70
Lined Inner Envelopes	LENV	4.90	9.80	14.70	19.60	4.90

Pricing includes black raised lettering and 14 lines of wording. For colored inks, add $7.00 to the TOTAL price of each item. Additional lines are $1.50 each.

Soft White (B)

ITEM	ITEM #	25	50	75	100	Add'l 25
Invitation	WFE241	65.90	67.90	69.90	71.90	15.30
Informal Note	WF2411	43.90	44.90	45.90	46.90	10.00
Reception	WF2413	43.90	44.90	45.90	46.90	10.00
Respond	WF2414	53.90	54.90	55.90	56.90	12.20
Printed Outer Envelopes	PENV	22.00	23.00	26.70	30.40	3.70
Lined Inner Envelopes	LENV	4.90	9.80	14.70	19.60	4.90

Pricing includes black raised lettering and 14 lines of wording. For colored inks, add $7.00 to the TOTAL price of each item. Additional lines are $1.50 each.

TRADITIONS OF THE HEART ▶

Three crisp panels are embossed one after the other to form a refined frame on this heavy card. The rich ecru card features your wording printed within the panels. Informals fold; reception and response enclosures are non-folding cards. Lined inner envelopes available: black (shown), gold, hunter, pearl, rosewood and wine. Displayed with wording W61 in black ink and lettering style QIL

SIZE: 5 1/8" x 7 1/4"

ITEM	ITEM #	25	50	75	100	Add'l 25
Invitation	WFJ099	70.90	72.90	74.90	76.90	16.30
Informal Note	WF5991	38.90	39.90	40.90	41.90	8.90
Reception	WF2993	38.90	39.90	40.90	41.90	8.90
Respond	WF2994	48.90	49.90	50.90	51.90	11.10
Printed Outer Envelopes	PENV	22.00	23.00	26.70	30.40	3.70
Lined Inner Envelopes	LENV	4.90	9.80	14.70	19.60	4.90

Pricing includes black raised lettering and 14 lines of wording. For colored inks, add $7.00 to the TOTAL price of each item. Additional lines are $1.50 each.

◀ HEART STRINGS

Pearl-embossed cherubs tug at the "heart strings" of this beautiful ecru invitation! The Z-fold is made of Forever Floral paper, which is richly embossed with an all-over pattern of rosebuds. A p[...] of floral hearts is embossed in pearl, delicately cut from the fold and printed with your first nam[...] Your wording appears when the invitation is opened. **Please specify names to be printed or we will use the first names from your inside wording.** Lined inner envelope available: gold and pe[...] Shown with wording W36 in wine ink.

SIZE:7 1/4" x 5 1/8"

ITEM	ITEM #	25	50	75	100	Add'l 25
Invitation	WFJ342	130.90	132.90	134.90	136.90	29.10
Informal Note	WF3421	52.90	53.90	54.90	55.90	11.90
Reception	WF3423	52.90	53.90	54.90	55.90	11.90
Respond	WF3424	62.90	63.90	64.90	65.90	14.10
Printed Outer Envelopes	PENV	22.00	23.00	26.70	30.40	3.70
Lined Inner Envelopes	LENV	4.90	9.80	14.70	19.60	4.90

Pricing includes black raised lettering and 14 lines of wording. For colored inks, add $7.00 to the TOTAL price of each item. Additional lines are $1.50 each.

BRIDAL SPLENDOR ▶

Beautifully embossed with roses and winding filigree, this invitation evokes images of Victorian elegance. The graceful design encircles your wording on a fold of rich, smooth ecru paper. Available lined inner envelope colors: gold, hunter, pearl and wine (shown). Displayed with custom wording and wine ink and lettering style SRH

SIZE: 5" x 6 5/8"

ITEM	ITEM #	25	50	75	100	Add'l 25
Invitation	WFE618	65.90	67.90	69.90	71.90	15.30
Informal Note	WF6181	43.90	44.90	45.90	46.90	10.00
Reception	WF6183	43.90	44.90	45.90	46.90	10.00
Respond	WF6184	53.90	54.90	55.90	56.90	12.20
Printed Outer Envelopes	PENV	22.00	23.00	26.70	30.40	3.70
Lined Inner Envelopes	LENV	4.90	9.80	14.70	19.60	4.90

Pricing includes black raised lettering and 14 lines of wording. For colored inks, add $7.00 to the TOTAL price of each item. Additional lines are $1.50 each.

SHEER FLORAL

Hydrangeas and roses in soft pink, purple, gold and green are visible through the sheer white paper of this folded invitation. Your wording is printed on the front within a simple embossed border. **Because of the translucent quality of the paper, please allow for some natural variation in color. When writing on translucent paper, be sure to use permanent ink to prevent smearing.** Note: The inner envelopes included are bright white with pointed flaps. Lined inner envelopes available: black, gold, hunter, pearl, purple (shown), silver, teal and wine. Displayed with wording W132 in purple ink and lettering style BIC.
SIZE: 5 1/8" x 7 1/4"

ITEM	ITEM #	25	50	75	100	Add'l 25
Invitation	WFJ642	159.00	162.00	164.00	167.90	35.70
Informal Note	WF6421	54.90	55.90	56.90	57.90	12.30
Reception	WF6423	54.90	55.90	56.90	57.90	12.30
Respond	WF6424	64.90	65.90	66.90	67.90	14.50
Printed Outer Envelopes	PENV	22.00	23.00	26.70	30.40	3.70
Lined Inner Envelopes	LENV	4.90	9.80	14.70	19.60	4.90

Pricing includes black raised lettering and 14 lines of wording. For colored inks, add $7.00 to the TOTAL price of each item. Additional lines are $1.50 each.

TROPICAL ROMANCE ▶

Perfect for a wedding with a tropical location or theme, this Tea Length invitation card features pearl-embossed shells that form a heart at the top and a border at the bottom. The paper is bright white Forever Floral – the embossed rosebuds add an extra touch of romance. Your names are printed within the heart at the top. **Please specify names to be printed or we will use the first names from the inside wording.** Lined inner envelopes available: gold (shown) and pearl. Displayed with wording W2 in brown ink and lettering style UNR-BIC.
SIZE: 4" x 9 1/4"

ITEM	ITEM #	25	50	75	100	Add'l 25
Invitation	WFT179	116.90	118.90	120.90	122.90	26.10
Informal Note	WF1791	52.90	53.90	54.90	55.90	11.90
Reception	WF1793	52.90	53.90	54.90	55.90	11.90
Respond	WF1794	62.90	63.90	64.90	65.90	14.10
Printed Outer Envelopes	PENV	22.00	23.00	26.70	30.40	3.70
Lined Inner Envelopes	LENV	4.90	9.80	14.70	19.60	4.90

Pricing includes black raised lettering and 14 lines of wording. For colored inks, add $7.00 to the TOTAL price of each item. Additional lines are $1.50 each.

JOINED BY LOVE ▶

Your hearts are entwined forever – and the pair of interlocking gold foil hearts at the top of this invitation symbolize your emotions beautifully! The non-folding invitation is made of sheer, bright white paper. An embossed panel at the edges further distinguishes your wording. Because of the translucent quality of the paper, please allow for some natural color variation. When writing on translucent paper, be sure to use permanent ink to prevent smearing. Lined inner envelopes available: black, gold (shown), hunter, pearl, periwinkle, purple, red, silver, teal and wine. Shown with wording W46 in gold ink and lettering style VOL.

SIZE: 5 1/8" x 7 1/4"

ITEM	ITEM #	25	50	75	100	Add'l 25
Invitation	WFJ1401	114.90	116.90	118.90	120.90	25.70
Informal Note	WF24011	54.90	55.90	56.90	57.90	12.30
Reception	WF24013	54.90	55.90	56.90	57.90	12.30
Respond	WF24014	64.90	65.90	66.90	67.90	14.50
Printed Outer Envelopes	PENV	22.00	23.00	26.70	30.40	3.70
Lined Inner Envelopes	LENV	4.90	9.80	14.70	19.60	4.90

Pricing includes black raised lettering and 14 lines of wording. For colored inks, add $7.00 to the TOTAL price of each item. Additional lines are $1.50 each.

QUAINT HYDRANGEA

A beautiful periwinkle blue hydrangea printed on a folded, sheer white insert is framed by an embossed window on the front of the bright white folded wrap. Your wording is printed inside sheer insert. You simply join the two-piece invitation with the pretied silver cord, which is incl Lined inner envelopes available: gold, pearl, purple and silver. Displayed with wording W132 i periwinkle ink and lettering style PEN.

SIZE: 5" x 6 5/8"

ITEM	ITEM #	25	50	75	100	Add'l 25
Invitation	WFE874	161.00	164.00	167.00	170.90	36.30
Informal Note	WF8741	43.90	44.90	45.90	46.90	10.00
Reception	WF8743	43.90	44.90	45.90	46.90	10.00
Respond	WF8744	53.90	54.90	55.90	56.90	12.20
Printed Outer Envelopes	PENV	22.00	23.00	26.70	30.40	3.70
Lined Inner Envelopes	LENV	4.90	9.80	14.70	19.60	4.90

Pricing includes black raised lettering and 14 lines of wording. For colored inks, add $7.00 to the TOTAL price of each item. Additional lines are $1.50 each.

UNIQUELY SWEET ▶

Silver foil hearts entwine at the top of this invitation, sending a message of true love. The invitation is made from sheer, bright white paper embossed with a crisp single panel. When writing on translucent paper, be sure to use permanent ink to prevent smearing. Lined inner envelopes available: black, hunter, pearl, periwinkle, purple, red, silver (shown), teal and wine. Displayed with wording W46 in silver ink and lettering style BIC.

SIZE: 5 1/8" x 7 1/4"

ITEM	ITEM #	25	50	75	100	Add'l 25
Invitation	WFJ187	114.90	116.90	118.90	120.90	25.70
Informal Note	WF1871	54.90	55.90	56.90	57.90	12.30
Reception	WF1873	54.90	55.90	56.90	57.90	12.30
Respond	WF1874	64.90	65.90	66.90	67.90	14.50
Printed Outer Envelopes	PENV	22.00	23.00	26.70	30.40	3.70
Lined Inner Envelopes	LENV	4.90	9.80	14.70	19.60	4.90

Pricing includes black raised lettering and 14 lines of wording. For colored inks, add $7.00 to the TOTAL price of each item. Additional lines are $1.50 each.

CLASSIC TRADITION IN ECRU

A single panel is embossed on a fold of rich ecru paper for a traditional invitation with impeccable style. Choose from three sizes to suit the style of your celebration. The matching reception and respond enclosures are unique non-folding cards. Invitations include tissues, unlined inner envelopes and blank outer envelopes. Respond cards include printed return envelopes. Note paper and thank you note folders include blank envelopes. Prices are for black ink. For a colorful ink, add $7.00 to the total price of each printed item.

A) ON THE INVITATION:
Lettering Style #299
Black Ink
Printed Return Envelope

A) LINER CHOICES:
Gold, Pearl, Taupe
SIZE: 5 1/8" x 7 5/16"

ITEM A	ITEM NUMBER	25	50	75	100	125	150	Add'l 25
Invitation	0IA-W23W	52.90	57.90	62.90	66.90	82.30	97.70	15.40
Printed Invitation Envelope Flaps	0IA-ERJO	22.90	26.90	28.90	30.90	35.40	39.90	4.50
Lined Inner Envelopes	Specify Color	4.90	9.80	14.70	19.60	24.50	29.40	4.90
Reception Folder	0IA-W9999R	35.90	37.90	39.90	41.90	51.10	60.30	9.20
Respond Folder	0IA-W9999E	43.90	45.90	47.90	49.90	60.90	71.90	11.00
Informal Notes	0IA-W400N	35.90	37.90	39.90	41.90	51.10	60.30	9.20
Thank You Folder – Blank Inside	0IA-W400T	35.90	37.90	39.90	41.90	51.10	60.30	9.20
Thank You Folder – Printed Inside	0IA-W400T2	56.40	58.40	66.60	74.80	90.20	105.60	15.40
Printed Envelope Flaps	0IA-ER200	22.90	26.90	28.90	30.90	35.40	39.90	4.50

CLASSIC TRADITION IN ECRU

ngle panel is embossed on a fold of rich ecru paper for a traditional invitation with eccable style. Choose from three sizes to suit the style of your celebration. The matching ption and respond enclosures are unique non-folding cards. Invitations include tissues, ned inner envelopes and blank outer envelopes. Respond cards include printed return elopes. Note paper and thank you note folders include blank envelopes. Prices are for k ink. For a colorful ink, add $7.00 to the total price of each printed item.

ON THE INVITATION:
ering Style #001
k Ink

B) LINER CHOICES:
Gold, Pearl
SIZE: A 5" x 6 5/8"

ON THE INVITATION:
ering Style #059
Ink

C) LINER CHOICE:
Gold (shown)
SIZE: B 4 7/16" x 5 13/16"

	ITEM NUMBER	25	50	75	100	125	150	Add'l 25
on Invitation	0IA-W43W	50.90	55.90	60.90	64.90	79.80	94.70	14.90
e Flaps	0IA-EREO	22.90	26.90	28.90	30.90	35.40	39.90	4.50
nner Envelopes	Specify Color	4.90	9.80	14.70	19.60	24.50	29.40	4.90
on Folder	0IA-W9999R	35.90	37.90	39.90	41.90	51.10	60.30	9.20
d Folder	0IA-W9999E	43.90	45.90	47.90	49.90	60.90	71.90	11.00
l Notes	0IA-W400N	35.90	37.90	39.90	41.90	51.10	60.30	9.20
ou Folder Inside	0IA-W400T	35.90	37.90	39.90	41.90	51.10	60.30	9.20
ou Folder d Inside	0IA-W400T2	56.40	58.40	66.60	74.80	90.20	105.60	15.40
Envelope Flaps	0IA-ER200	22.90	26.90	28.90	30.90	35.40	39.90	4.50

	ITEM NUMBER	25	50	75	100	125	150	Add'l 25
on Invitation	0IA-W11W	43.90	47.90	51.90	55.90	68.80	81.70	12.90
e Flaps	0IA-ERDO	22.90	26.90	28.90	30.90	35.40	39.90	4.50
nner Envelopes	Specify Color	4.90	9.80	14.70	19.60	24.50	29.40	4.90
on Folder	0IA-W9999R	35.90	37.90	39.90	41.90	51.10	60.30	9.20
d Folder	0IA-W9999E	43.90	45.90	47.90	49.90	60.90	71.90	11.00
l Notes	0IA-W400N	35.90	37.90	39.90	41.90	51.10	60.30	9.20
ou Folder Inside	0IA-W400T	35.90	37.90	39.90	41.90	51.10	60.30	9.20
ou Folder d Inside	0IA-W400T2	56.40	58.40	66.60	74.80	90.20	105.60	15.40
Envelope Flaps	0IA-ER200	22.90	26.90	28.90	30.90	35.40	39.90	4.50

www.YourBridalSuperstore.com

The items found in this catalog are just a small sample
of the thousands of products at:

YourBridalSuperstore.com

The Ultimate Online Wedding Source

See and compare the largest selection of beautiful and unique
wedding products not available at your local bridal boutiques:

Jewelry	Accessories
Stationery	Invitations
Gifts	Favors

YourBridalSuperstore.com is an invaluable resource to help
you make the best decision when choosing all your wedding
products.

Look for special offers, new products, sale items and more
when you log onto:

www.YourBridalSuperstore.com

YOUR BRIDAL SUPERSTORE
The Ultimate Online Wedding Source℠
www.YourBridalSuperstore.com

We provide unparalleled customer service, highest quality
products, lowest price guarantee, and free shipping.*

FREE OFFER!

*Limited time only

Receive a fabulous wedding gift (valued over $30) and a $10.00
gift certificate when you visit *www.YourBridalSuperstore.com*.

To receive this offer, log onto
www.YourBridalSuperstore.com/offerewwo.htm

Offering the largest selection of wedding accessories,
invitations, jewelry, gifts, and more.

*Log onto *www.YourBridalSuperstore.com* for details.